A Radical Romance

A Radical Romance

A Memoir of Love, Grief and Consolation

ALISON LIGHT

FIG TREE
an imprint of
PENGUIN BOOKS

FIG TREE

UK | USA | Canada | Ireland | Australia
India | New Zealand | South Africa

Fig Tree is part of the Penguin Random House group of companies
whose addresses can be found at global.penguinrandomhouse.com.

First published 2019
001

Every effort has been made to trace copyright holders and to obtain their
permission for the use of copyright material. The publisher apologizes for any
errors or omissions and would be grateful to be notified of any corrections
that should be incorporated in future editions of this book

Typeset in 12.5/15.75 pt Bembo Book MT Std
by Integra Software Services Pvt. Ltd, Pondicherry
Printed and bound in Great Britain by Clays Ltd, Elcograf S.p.A.

A CIP catalogue record for this book is available from the British Library

ISBN: 978–0–241–24450–0

www.greenpenguin.co.uk

Penguin Random House is committed to a
sustainable future for our business, our readers
and our planet. This book is made from Forest
Stewardship Council® certified paper.

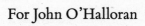

For John O'Halloran

Contents

Preface: Love and History

In the summer of 1955, when I was born, Raphael fell in love. Or rather 'Ralph' did. He had changed his name when recruiting for the St Pancras branch of the British Communist Party, because the London comrades said they couldn't pronounce it. He was twenty and Jean, his inamorata, was eighteen. Both came from 'Party' families (the Communist Party was always the 'Party' with a capital 'P'), though Jean had joined only that spring. They met at the headquarters of the British Communist Party in King Street, Covent Garden, in the underground room where student gatherings were held. Ralph was about to begin his final year reading history at Oxford and Jean to start a history degree at St Andrews in Scotland. As the universities were five hundred miles apart, they relied on letters; telephoning, in those days of public call boxes, was more difficult. A few months later they got engaged.

When I met Raphael in the mid 1980s, he told me about his first fiancée; she came to our wedding party and we are still in touch. Raphael was a familiar figure by then on the British Left, with a reputation as a radical historian and as the founder of the History Workshop movement, but I knew little about his past. He was in the middle of writing a series of articles for *New Left Review* reflecting on his youth and on 'the lost world' of the British Communist Party. He gave me copies. All lovers share their histories but this was too much information too soon. I merely skimmed the pieces, concentrating on the personal bits. 'I'm glad you didn't know me then,' he would say. His early incarnation as Ralph, for whom politics was everything, made him squirm. Raphael had wanted to write a further article based on his letters to Jean, which she had kept. In due course, like a good comrade, she sent them, but he never got any further than a few sketchy notes.

I found Raphael's letters to Jean and his notes when I was sorting through the mounds of files, papers, books and materials in our Spitalfields home after his death. I was hoping to establish an archive of his work but I also wanted to clear his study, turn it into a sitting room, and not have to confront his absence every time I walked into the house. I put the letters to one side. I could not bring myself to read them. Not, I'm afraid, because of any qualms I had about intruding on other people's privacy. I expected these letters to be largely concerned with Party matters. But Raphael and I had also conducted our courtship by correspondence from different cities. In the throes of grief I was not in the mood for parallels or comparisons, no matter how dry and distant.

Fast-forward another twenty years, and, with this memoir in mind, I encounter the letters again as I go through the boxes I still have. These boxes have travelled with me in my widowhood from London to Newcastle and on to Oxford. Jean is living down the road and we meet up for a walk in the University Parks. She comes down hard on her earlier political commitments: 'We were children then, children,' she insists. And I wonder to myself how Raphael would have talked or written of his past had he too lived to be a spry octogenarian.

In his notes for his articles in the 1980s, Raphael was looking for evidence of what he called, in Marx's terms, the 'species-being' of a young Communist in the Britain of the 1950s, self-consciously recognizing what he shared with other members of the Party. 'Ralph' was to be an example of a psyche shaped by 'some thirteen years of CP formation' (Raphael deemed himself a Communist at the age of eight). There was little to recommend them as letters, he thought – that is, as literary artefacts fashioned for a reader. They are 'emotionally monotonous' and censorious. They made him 'wince'. 'The humour,' he wrote, 'strikes me as leaden'; the letters 'have no eloquence, no guile, no surprise'. Although he conceded that 'the person who wrote them seems to have a low view of his abilities and to be without personal conceit', this he felt 'was a trick of self-presentation' (so some guile after all?).

It is true that the letters are mostly digests or reports of the sort that might appeal only to the historian of political movements or to the cognoscenti; much is doctrinaire. Here was the young ideologue analysing the news from the Party's British mouthpiece, the *Daily Worker*, scrawling sixteen or seventeen pages every couple of days – *twenty-three* on the resignation of Clement Attlee, the British prime minister, a letter which nonetheless ends 'in haste'. Here are the minutiae of branch meetings, the sagas of days and nights spent recruiting – 'I hammered away at him,' Ralph writes of one hapless soul he was 'working on' – the detail of campaigns, study groups, rallies and demonstrations, canvassing for signatures and organizing rallies or demonstrations. Much is couched in sectarian Party terms, and 'the pedagogic strain' is indeed, as Raphael laments in his notes, 'absolutely consistent'. Young Ralph had spent two of his three years at Oxford on work for the Party. Now he was determined to get a first-class degree, since it behoved Party members to prove their intellectual worth. He becomes Jean's long-distance tutor, sending her reading lists to counter the insularity of the history degrees they both have to endure. He offers all manner of political advice. The tone of his letters seems immeasurably fuddy-duddy in these days before the idea of a youth culture hit Britain. Ralph is a twenty-year-old going on forty.

So why do I find 'Ralph' so appealing? He seems to me no more lacking in self-knowledge than most self-absorbed young men. I find him funny too. 'My letters to you all seem to be the accurate reflection of the Complete Bore,' Ralph confesses. 'This has been worrying me quite a lot recently.' Despite their conscious intentions, the letters are shot through with longing – they *are* love letters, from someone all too obviously in the grip of intense passions which cannot be controlled. Though headed only 'Thursday' or 'Sunday', their sequence can be as easily dated by the escalating endearments as by the unfolding events in the Communist world. A first letter in autumn 1955 begins 'Dear Jean' and is signed, somewhat ambiguously, 'many friendly and other fraternal greetings, Ralph Samuel'. Gradually the address warms to 'darling' or 'sweetheart', with 'cheerio' and even 'love' by way of farewell. The last few culminate in 'dearest sweetheart' and 'all my love'.

Ralph is in love and his world is gloriously transfigured. He wants to talk to everyone about Jean, to learn everything Scottish, and he drags Scotland into every conversation at the drop of a hat (or a tam-o'-shanter). He even affects a sentimental Scottish accent, using 'wee' in the letters. She is perfect, radiant, the ideal object of his affections. He is beset by fears before their next meeting. What if she goes under a bus? He bombards her with letters and she tries to slow him down. When Jean is overwhelmed, he vows, 'I promise to write less,' and 'to stay extrovert'. Much in the letters evokes a familiar courtship dance: advance, retreat, advance, retreat. Surely 'don't write to me of love' has been the woman's defensive cry throughout the ages as she feels herself besieged?

But we fall in love in history, in our particular time. For young Communists, 'staying extrovert' also meant being 'Party-minded', suppressing personal needs for the sake of the cause. To be a Communist was, in theory at least, a complete social identity. Under Communism there was to be no private life. In 1956 Ralph's ambition was to be a Party organizer and Jean seemed an ideal comrade to share this future. Together they hitchhiked across the country to meet and to attend political rallies and recruit new members. Ralph's romantic ideal was the making of 'the good Communist home', where work and love would be indivisible. (Years later, in our own marriage, he remembered being moved by portraits of Lenin and his wife, Krupskaya, which showed him at his desk and her reading companionably nearby in an armchair.)

Ralph and Jean's engagement was short-lived. The events of 1956 proved too much for them and for their political beliefs: the Twentieth Congress of the Communist Party, where the extent of Stalin's crimes was revealed and denounced; Suez; the Soviet invasion of Hungary; and the pusillanimous refusal of the British Communist Party to express any regret at their uncritical acceptance of the past policies of the Soviet leadership or to countenance discussion of democratic changes. Both Raphael and Jean left the Party and their romance collapsed.

★

Reading Ralph's letters, I thought I recognized the sense of urgency, the erudition, the relentless commitment to work and the extravagance of expression. But I could only have married the older man who had other incarnations, other lovers. In the mid 1950s Raphael did not live with Jean McCrindle, as he was to with Anna Davin, his partner and co-worker in the early 1970s, bringing up her three children with her. By then 'the struggle' – a socialist politics which put class and economic analysis first and foremost – was being questioned by new social movements. Raphael helped run the crèche at the first British Women's Liberation conference, which was held at Ruskin College in Oxford in 1967; he learnt to share the housework, the cooking and the shopping. Living and working with feminists changed his ideas of what history was and of where power resided. None of this happened overnight, but I was glad, as I used to say, that he had been 'done over' by the time I met him.

I might have encountered Raphael when I was a student (he would have been about forty then). Fran, my closest friend at college, mentioned she was going to a History Workshop, a gathering of historians with an interest in what was called 'people's history' or 'history from below', which was Raphael's brainchild, but I didn't much like the sound of it. I had done my best to avoid 'the novels of industrialization' during my English degree, and had little interest then in the history of the labouring or working classes. That past was still my present, too close to home, not yet 'my background'. I could not have made my grandparents or my parents an object of study. So I didn't see Raphael coming and our paths never crossed.

I cannot make my life tally with Raphael's – our differences are also what brought us together – but I do feel the reader needs something of my past, since I was not a tabula rasa when we met. Here and there, and especially at the start of the book, I pick out themes from my imaginary autobiography, were I to write it, and reflect on what we saw in each other. Looking back at my younger self, which really means inventing a version of my younger self, I am struck by how readily I patronize my youth. Perhaps I am disheartened to find that much of what I now think was already there and not only in embryo. Having any kind of new thought is much harder than one thinks. It may be that we only get to know our old thoughts better, whether we accept or reject them.

When I met Raphael he was historicizing himself, turning his self into history. The articles on his Communist past, published in 1985–6, were partly prompted by the miners' strike and the attempts of Prime Minister Margaret Thatcher's government to decimate trade-union power in Britain. The miners' strike was also at the heart of a debate about class and about what class feeling and class belonging might mean for a British Left at what felt like the end of an era of industrial socialism. Raphael saw himself as belonging to an earlier age of mass social movements. His articles have since become part of a much wider discussion about the British Communist Party and its peculiarities. How much was Raphael, especially in his autobiographical approach, evoking a 'species-being', or simply his own singularity? Was he truly representative?

These are questions for historians but they are also questions about the nature of memoir and the kind of history that it gives us, a history from inside. Memoir weaves its way between what is often called the private and the public, the personal as opposed to the historical. I have called this book a

memoir for want of any other term. I find these terms far
more porous than absolute. They seep into each other. This is
not a biography of Raphael; nor is it my autobiography.
Things will look different in another twenty years' time. In
part I am writing a homage, a tribute to a man whom I knew
to be a good and rare human being; in part a love story and a
death story, and a story about a marriage and its vicissitudes.
If it is also a story about politics, then 'the political', for me
at least, was not a matter of parliament and party, or the
shenanigans of Westminster politicians, but how I encountered
it through Raphael, and found what was meaningful to me.
Others will not see this as very political at all.

★

Memoirs are still rarely written by the wives; those that are
tend to appear in the first few years of a bereavement. A
widow, especially one quite long in the tooth like me, is in a
peculiar position. How can I restore the mystery and sepa-
rateness to the person, turn them back into the pieces they
were before I assumed I could fit them together? The poet
P. J. Kavanagh writes in *The Perfect Stranger*, his tender account
of his own lost love, that 'we have only the bits and pieces of
ourselves' with which to celebrate another person. This memoir is my own kaleidoscope.

Memoir plays fast and loose with time. The inner life and
the outer go at different speeds, or paces; they have different
temporalities from clock time. Looking back over twenty-
odd years, what seems as compelling to me are those times
when the story of our selves seizes up, when there is no progress, and when we realize, if only in glimpses, that we are

not in control. Childhood, falling in love, illness, old age –
these are times out of time. Mourning is another.

Mourning works like a leaven in a life and it never stops
working. It is formative, or it was for me. At forty-one, childless, I was out of sync with friends and family. But I am old
enough now to recognize this condition as a theme or pattern, a way of thinking about myself, familiar from
childhood, both lonely and freeing. Like all the bereaved, I
have had particular work to do at different times. I have had
to learn how to incorporate the dead into my life without
becoming a monument to grief. In that time I have done a
fair bit of what I call 'widowing about'. I edited two volumes
of Raphael's essays, spent several years establishing an archive
of his papers, and have been part of the research centre set up
in his name. So why do I want to write about him now? I feel
old enough, would be one way of putting it, or equal to it.
Though perhaps I mean, and the thought surprises me, that I
feel equal to him. I was no ingénue or neophyte when we
met, but I got used to being seen as young, even precocious.
However much we shared, the age difference meant that we
could never be peers. When I began writing this book I was
the same age – sixty-one – as Raphael was when he died;
another generation has grown up, and my second marriage
has already lasted longer than the first. I've written my own
books and can more easily acknowledge Raphael as a mentor,
though as a strict egalitarian he would doubtless have said
that I was his.

As a historian, Raphael had more past in his life than most.
Not least, what weighed on me personally, the body of his
work, which filled our entire house over five floors. Throughout my mourning I wanted two opposite, impossible things: to

hold on tightly and belligerently to absolutely everything, and to be free of it all at one stroke. The fear of being overwhelmed by the past is matched by the fear that there will be nothing left to show for a life. Mourning lurches between the compulsion to remember and the desire – at times far more frightening – to forget utterly. More frightening, perhaps, because it heralds our own mortality, our eventual absorption into history.

Raphael was well known in his day, not film-star famous, not a 'celebrity', but a charismatic figure on the British Left for more than thirty years. He was a writer whose prose was vivid and accessible, often witty and elegant. He took part in debates on television and radio and he wrote frequently for the press, engaging with public issues – on the place of history in the national curriculum, for instance. His voice, the voice of the public intellectual and the engaged, critical historian, is still missed; in an age of instant opinion, such voices are in short supply. Writing this memoir, I have had to resist the urge to ventriloquize or to be his amanuensis. I do not give an account of his work, though I hope the memoir will whet the reader's appetite to read more of it.

As Raphael's life and his different worlds have become history, a curious reversal is happening in my own. When I meet younger people and talk about my and Raphael's life together, I start to feel as if I am making it up: so I want to write about him to make him real again. I am more struck these days by the comedy of two people coming together, of love and marriage as a human comedy. My marriage with Raphael often makes me smile now, even laugh, but that levity is a way of lightening the weight of the past. It is not satirical, I hope, or fey, but an attempt at sharing understanding – laughing with, not at – a saving grace which is ultimately freeing. That too is the point of writing.

Since I began this book a number of people have asked me, 'Is it harder to write now that you are married again?' I have translated this as 'Might John [my second husband] mind?' The romantic fantasy that we can love only one person in the world – a soulmate, 'Mr Right' – is alive and well. The fact that it is a fantasy does not make it any less powerful. But if we could love only once, how bleak our lives would be!

Love and history. Reading Ralph's letters to Jean, I am touched, not by the lost youth, but by the longings between the lines. That a person goes on wanting to be other and different, despite political orthodoxies or the conventions of their upbringing; despite, as it were, who they think they are or ought to be. Love, the French historian Jules Michelet once famously wrote, is history's protest. Without romance, how might we move towards each other, attracted by what we don't have, what we need and admire, as much as by what we share? The 'romantic' speaks to the transcendent, to dreams and visions, and to what poets call the imagination – to what we do not yet know we are longing for. It can also be a sign of our discontent with what society has to offer. It speaks to those who believe that an inner change must accompany and foment any social transformation. How to achieve this without coercion? That is the question.

In our years together, what we called Raphael's 'Communist unconscious' would often surface. One night early on in our courtship, talking in his sleep, he woke me and said, 'But, darling, the working class is advancing across the globe.' That lost world of faith and of looking hopefully to the future, now so discredited, had become a deep reach of his inner life, repressed, taboo and full of pleasure. Who was he arguing with if not another part of himself? And why do I still remember this dream and treasure it? Because it delighted me and we both laughed at its apparent guilelessness. Yes. And because it was given to *me*. I was woken up to receive it, felt cheered by it, me the Portsmouth girl who had lost her footing in her own class. That idealism lifted my spirits, an optimism whose history stretches back over the centuries and a belief that human beings can change their lives for the better, seeing beyond the narrow orbit of their selves. Consolation lies in the hope, as in the romance.

Prologue

The wooden staircase led down to the kitchen. Leaning at forty-five degrees, and with one hand balanced on the wainscoting, I turned the brass door knob, and the glass-panelled door swung inwards, almost colliding with the bench under the kitchen table. The table and some dark wood chairs were truncated, as if in an infant school classroom, because the ceiling was so low. Apart from the red-tiled floor, the room was entirely wooden; all the walls were matchboarded in old pine, varnished or painted off-white, though this, like the ceiling, was liberally seasoned with nicotine. So closely cabined did it feel, we might have been on board ship, in the captain's quarters perhaps, and on a stormy night expect the table to slide across the floor if it was not bolted down. Although there was hardly room for four to sit comfortably, the kitchen somehow expanded to accommodate a meeting of a dozen or more. It was also where Raphael, his hand constantly pushing away the swatch of hair that fell across his face, cooked elaborate and deeply unpunctual meals, including one memorable experiment with an East End delicacy, eel pie. After he had tasted it, so the story goes, he announced with mock solemnity, 'Comrades, I must withdraw this dish.'

In my memory it is always evening there, perhaps because the basement kitchen never saw the sun or because our first passionate embrace took place on that very threshold, the bottom step of the stairs, after a late supper, exotic to me, of grilled cheese and fennel; or perhaps such memories are best suited to a half-light. The kitchen's Rembrandtian glow owed much to the rich gleam of wood but it was also due, I discovered, to the low-wattage light bulbs that Raphael favoured over *more stark illumination. The softening effect was forgiving of the house's age and imperfections, as if it were an elderly woman concerned with her looks and choosing to position herself with her back to the daylight. In the chiaroscuro I could find myself, in years to come, disconcertingly out of time. Sitting in the fireside chair, its brown velvet seat suitably worn and its basket weave frayed, I would gaze out of the two small windows into the London dark, watching the ankles and feet going past on the pavement outside. Only the sight of Raphael's suede desert boots would startle me back to the present.*

Where was Spitalfields? When I lived in the capital a few years previously, I had heard of its fruit-and-veg market on the fringe of the East End, but Liverpool Street station was my ultima Thule. *Apart from one trip to Petticoat Lane to hear the barkers flogging their tea towels and dodgy watches, I had hardly visited it. Now, coming up from Brighton for my first encounter with the reading group, I took the yellow Circle Line from Victoria, and emerged in the thick of rush hour on the corner of Broad Street. The main-line station was a baffling arrangement of parapets and stairs; women in high heels, dressed for the office, their shoulder pads as broad as an American footballer's, and men in suits and ties hurried past me as I made for the lit windows of the Great Eastern Hotel, where other commuters were busy drowning the day's sorrows before heading home to Chelmsford or Clapton.*

I crossed over Bishopsgate, weaving between the taxis and the red double-deckers, past the news-stand where the vendor cried out the late final, and went left, heading out of the City. Past the cavernous entrance to Dirty Dicks wine bar and the blue lamp of the police station, past the crenellated towers of the Bishopsgate Institute, and soon the traffic and the people began to thin out. Spital Square, on my right, was hushed and hidden behind local shops, though I could see the green-and-white ironwork of the covered market in the distance. Everything was shut – Dewhurst the butcher's, a print shop and a post office, and the travel company where I turned into Folgate Street, its scarlet neon sign for a 'Polyglot Agency' flickering like an eerie beacon. In later years Raphael and I were half convinced the business was a front for MI6.

I used to dream of Spitalfields more than I ever did of Raphael, in the tormented months of early widowhood. The tall, narrow houses looming over each other, the shadowy alleyways and courts, featured as the monochrome backdrop to a landscape of anxiety and menace, part Fritz Lang, part Hollywood noir, where I wandered distraught. But when I first went there it was a peaceful backwater, a little derelict and unkempt, but not the place of nightmare. Lined with bollards from the days of horse-drawn traffic, the streets were barely wide enough for cars. Footsteps reverberated on cobbles. There were no proper pavements, only stretches of pitted concrete and asphalt; the lighting was patchy. It was certainly very built-up: no greenery, back or front gardens. Elder Street, like its neighbour Blossom Street, was bereft of trees.

At first sight, number 19, with its flaking stucco, its lace curtains shrouding the windows, seemed equally sequestered. I was welcomed into a hall lit by an electric chandelier made from an old gas fitting, the short passageway of bare, polished wood lined with floor-to-ceiling shelves. Loose papers, pamphlets, journals, books of every age, binding and condition, and black lever-arch A3 files, perched precariously on the polished treads of the staircase, winding out of sight; they lay in drifts on the floor of Raphael's study, next to the front door, the only room on the ground floor. Arriving early for the meeting, I was invited to sit there and read while Raphael worked at his paper-strewn desk. Feeling self-conscious in a lumpy armchair draped with an itchy orange cover of unknown provenance and age, I rested my feet on a battered leather stool, its horsehair spilling out. A defunct cast-iron stove spanned the fireplace, serving as another bookshelf. With its faded

Turkish rug, dark maroon panelling and heavy brocade curtains, the room felt like a retreat. Only the telephone struck a modern note. Even the anglepoise lamps were curiously fashioned from antique fitments, and all the surfaces of the bookshelves and built-in filing cupboards were finished with green baize felt, of the sort that once insulated the door to the servants' quarters in grander houses, or covered a billiards table, though the tobacco that hung in the air came from Raphael's incessant roll-ups and not from a gentleman's cigar.

I had never known anyone choose to live with so many old things – too many, far too many, for me to do more than register them at random. Prints and pictures covered the walls: obscure political caricatures with balloons coming out of their mouths, uttering gibes and witticisms once thought biting; solemn engravings of dignified quarry men or navvies; London characters – its watermen and dust collectors – etched in grey and green, and Bartholomew Fair seething with a vast crowd under a turbulent sky (but these last I can picture easily because I still have them). Mantelpieces were cluttered with old postcards and memorabilia: a plate commemorating Gladstone; a statuette of Wesley. Over the kitchen cupboards an array of assorted crockery was displayed, cream-coloured with age, and pewter jugs on hooks, whose effect, when I got my eye in, suggested more the snug of a country inn than the cabin of my nautical imagination. The venerable wall clock, though, encased in a round metal cylinder like a barometer, had once belonged to a ship. Always running slow or fast, it now never keeps the time in my own study.

That first time in Raphael's house, if I had been asked to give my impressions, I would probably have called it all 'Dickensian', 'period', the feel of a nineteenth-century past, or of pastness itself. The place, like its inhabitant, was eccentric and intriguing; somewhat overwhelming. Downstairs I would have looked about me, greeted the others, accepted a glass of red wine and a wedge of cheese. Most likely

I was preoccupied with our forthcoming discussion. If the spirit of the future had appeared to me then, I would have stood amazed, perhaps even quailed at the prospect before me. Elder Street, she would announce brightly, would be my home for fifteen years, familiar, loved and hated. Courtship and marriage were around the corner. Raphael – but perhaps here she would have saved me too much foreknowledge. That first night, though, I heard only the ghost of past times whispering, a vague, dissonant chorus. In any case, I had another life waiting and would soon be on the late train back to Brighton. I'd wake up next morning fifty miles away in my flat, with its long strip of garden and its far-off horizon of glittering sea.

Meeting

1   Stops and Starts

Those who listen to a life story, be they adepts – the psycho-analyst, oral historian or professional interviewer – or simply a friend or passing stranger, soon learn that it obscures as much as it reveals. Its incidents and highlights, related many times, have become a series of *tableaux vivants* that seem illuminating to the teller but are so firmly fixed in place that nothing else can be seen – to the left or right or behind – and all the stage machinery, by which I mean the operations of memory, the peculiar processes that have sum-moned forth and selected these scenes and not others, are hidden. Anyone seriously intent on knowing more of a per-son must probe and question, irritate them or make them laugh, until some of that easy fall-back on remembered memories starts to falter; the scenery, the backdrop of the *mise en scène*, begins to tremble, and the paraphernalia of the production – a chaotic congregation of actors, stagehands, lights, props and costumes – is glimpsed. So it is with the autobiographer who tells stories to herself that she has long since turned into her self.

Memory is, in other words, and as we all now know, the least trustworthy of witnesses. What we remember, or think we do, shifts with the passing of time – the preternatural capacity of the elderly to recall fine details of childhood being the most obvious example of memory's elasticity. What we remember is never simply a matter of volition: memories, we say, are 'triggered', or, less reactively, 'float up'; like dreams, they conflate past and present; they substitute one event or place for another, abbreviate or extend duration to impossible lengths, or they return over and again to some detail or scrap of reminiscence, with the obsessiveness of Dickens's Mr Dick and his King Charles's head. And we forget so much. If we are what we remember, how curious and touching and surprising it is that we have built our houses on such sand.

Yet writers have often turned memory's vicissitudes into virtues. Faced with its prestidigitation, they enjoy its tricks and hail the conjurer. Memory gives us different tonalities, those shades and colours of our inner life, so often at odds with the starkness of clock time. And, however fleeting, memory cherishes the lost, reanimates the dead and honours their place inside ourselves. Memory, they say, resists the bullying of chronology that sweeps us so heartlessly to the grave; it plays with time and plays for time, preferring the beautiful, poetic ambiguity of the image to the stark fact in a relentless plot. Though remembering may be painful, it appears to offer remission.

Perhaps all a memoirist can do, faced with the awful, actual formlessness of a life, is to hold its themes and repetitions up to the light, create a pattern from them, knowing full well that any design is a happy invention. And isn't that how we live our sense of our selves, in this oscillation between the fraying fabric of the present and the ravelled-up stories which shape time passing; a self that is never complete, always refashioned in the social world, and yet somehow feels to us necessarily and believably continuous?

★

If I were looking for one way of characterizing my life, I might choose stalling as a motif, the engine of my progress periodically cutting out. Stopping and starting again. In the breaks, in those lulls of animated suspension, between jobs, say, or between loves, I have felt in control, albeit temporarily. Retrospectively, of course, as in the false seamlessness of a curriculum vitae, my chopping and changing appears more as method than madness. I appear to have been decisive, and I did relish that feeling. But most of my decisions, especially in the years before I met Raphael, seemed to happen by default. I generally knew more what I didn't want than what I did; and I 'knew' it not in some bold, pioneering way but through feeling wretched or in a state of panic. Turning aside, not doing the next expected thing, flooded me with relief. I was out of the race.

Perhaps, in these pockets of stolen time, I was recapturing the need to abscond, to find boltholes as I used to when I was a small child, earmarking territories, inserting myself into crannies – the corner under the dado rail on the upstairs landing, or squeezing down behind the back of the sofa in the sitting room, or inside the hot tent of the clothes airing on the wooden clothes horse by the fire, the family's linen embracing me with its acrid smell. Or when I stepped off the hamster wheel of timetabled lessons at grammar school and was granted the privilege of studying alone for part of my A levels in the sanctuary of the Senior Library (a mixed blessing: it stoked the bullying I suffered from and encouraged my feelings of superiority). Perhaps, by then, in any case, I was already a veteran of solitude, an infant who had grown inured to being alone, coughing her way through the recurring bronchitis that saw her, most winters, propped up in the front bedroom, left to read and wool-gather. Did that deprivation become an appetite in later life? Who knows? When I took up therapy in my late twenties I was cheered by the idea that my changes of direction, usually in flight, were not detours or dropping out, but forays, attempts to become 'the author of my life'. Now I look on that as a flattering, if saving, fiction.

In my twenties I had a recurring dream. I dreamt that my sister, Sandra, said to me: 'You've always been a minder.' Not an accusation but a bald statement of ambiguous truth. A minder – someone who looks after things but also someone who 'minds', takes umbrage, perhaps, or who 'thinks too much', my mother's anxious put-down which haunted me for years. Thinking came from minding – from feeling and trying to make sense of those feelings (did I also 'feel too much'?). It was years before I asked the question 'Too much for whom?' I was a minder; I minded and I kept things in mind. When all else failed, my mind would have to do the job of looking after me.

If all my life I have needed to stall and to make room for what I thought was 'my self', this is an urge that stems at least in part, or so I like to believe, from the precarious pleasures of minding as much as I do. Now I am in my sixties, these hiatuses are a way of life. In other words, I like to tell myself that I became who I am, a writer, a teacher and an intellectual, accidentally on purpose. This may be camouflage, disguising my ambitions, and appealing to the reader as an innocent. I shall say next to nothing here of that other creature who emerged from the chrysalis of illness and solitude, the all-singing, all-dancing child who was also me, the child who loved to perform and to be applauded. But I realize she is the loner's sister, even her non-identical twin. Perhaps what matters are the forms that this tension takes in a human life, between hiding from the world and wanting to reach out to it, between the need to be recognized as singular and yet accepted as akin to everyone else.

So when I think of the mid 1980s, not long before I met Raphael, what comes to mind is an image. I see myself sitting in the sun on the low dividing wall in the garden of my flat in Brighton, gazing past the white ziggurat of the American Express building, over the rooftops of Kemptown to the glinting edge of the Channel. As if in a photograph, carefully composed, though one that was never taken. There is a domestic note: my cat, Morgan, perches serenely alongside at a companionable distance, like a small Buddha. A picture of peaceful contemplation, as if the view I am gazing at were offering a stable perspective on my life, the future all laid out before me, sunlit and open. I am taking another breather, ventilating the present.

I was proud of my flat two thirds of the way up Albion Hill, its incline so precipitous that, lumbering up with two bags of groceries from the London Road Sainsbury's, I used to feel as if my knuckles must be grazing the pavement. The flat was damp, unheated, and the carpet smelt, but it was purpose-built, the top half of the house, with its own front door. The stairs led up to a tiny kitchen, a front room and a back bedroom with a tacked-on bathroom extension. From the window over the street, if I leant sideways, I could glimpse the green slopes of the Sussex Downs. At the back, rickety wooden steps ran down to the garden. The far end abutted allotments while a brick wall, barely more than three feet high, separated my patch from a similar strip next door. Nothing grew there except grass and brambles. 'I'm terrified of the garden,' I wrote in my diary, knowing nothing of horticulture. But the garden, with its sweeping vista over the town and the sea on the far horizon, was also the flat's chief attraction; I wanted to sit in that garden, so I would have to learn to cultivate it.

Often in the years to come I was to find this image consoling – me on that garden wall in the sunshine. It is not surprising that it so lodged in my memory. Leafing through my diaries, I find I have evoked the scene several times, as a touchstone of sorts, an ideal. A fantasy of homeostasis, it is also, I see now, an image of division, conjuring a partition between past and present, between classes and cultures, between different ways of being men and women. In Brighton I was sitting on the fence.

I was back living on the south coast, halfway between my sister and her family to the east in Rye, and Portsmouth to the west, where the rest of the family lived. An area of huddled terraced streets, its landmarks the pub and the corner shop, this was the familiar territory of my growing up, as it had been of my mother's and my grandmother's, and back into the nineteenth century, when scores of these two-storey houses were built en masse all over Britain for the poorer sort. I had been born in such a house and now I found myself reliving old patterns. Everything and everyone was within walking distance. I went 'round' to see people or met them in the local pub (we were not then a café society); it was a short walk to the local cinema or to go shopping; at weekends I could stroll along the seafront, as I had throughout my adolescence.

I had not gone far geographically, but my tastes in food, music and clothes were increasingly unlike those of my upbringing. I might banter, as my mother did, with the postman and milkman, but my friends were from the university or worked in professional, salaried jobs. When I took my washing to the local launderette, the woman in charge told me she had brought up three children in my flat. I knew what that meant and why she smiled wistfully: my parents had begun their married life in similar circumstances; everyone we knew in the 1950s had been in the same boat, renting for a few shillings a week. Now I was one of a different breed, taking on a mortgage, as the old flats were sold off. I did not kid myself. I was 'Miss Light' to her.

In the 1880s the women on Albion Hill pegged out their washing and passed the time of day over the low back walls. A hundred years later, I got used to my downstairs neighbours, Michael, a hairdresser, and his boyfriend, Keith, wandering out in floral silk peignoirs to chat with me; and to joking with the blokes on the allotments at the far end, who advised me on the planting and the laying out of flower beds. Michael cut my hair; small gifts of tomatoes or potatoes would appear overnight on the bottom wall. The sociability suited me while I was working out a separate existence. But I was between worlds, as perhaps we always are.

★

I was approaching thirty when I met Raphael. I'd had several jobs, including school teaching and a permanent post at the BBC, and fallen in and out of love. In all I'd moved seven times, across Bedford, London and down to Brighton. When I left college I had no blueprint for the future. This must be pretty usual, if not one definition of youth, especially so in the mid 1970s, when jobs were thicker on the ground. But going to Cambridge University to read English at just eighteen had taken me into terra incognita, well beyond my ken. I had no sense of vocation, no footsteps to follow in, no money, and no prospect of it, to fall back on. I took heart from the comfort briskly offered by my Scottish tutor of medieval studies, Helena Shire. Visiting me when I was laid up with bronchitis in the college sickbay, she advised: 'It's not a carr-reer that matters but a *life!*' I wanted to have a *life* and in a Micawberish vein was sure something would turn up. I sent off applications for posts I didn't want and wasn't qualified for, the Civil Service and the Atomic Energy Authority among them, and collected rejections. I thought of leaving the country, and secured a Common-wealth Research Fellowship at UBC in Vancouver (I was infatuated with a good-looking Canadian postgrad at the time). I had barely been abroad and was not brave enough to take it up. So I did what girls did when they left college, and what I said I would never, ever do. I got engaged to be married.

We took a dingy flat in St Neots, halfway between Cam-bridge and Bedford, and via the university's career office I stumbled into a job teaching English and Latin at a boys' inde-pendent school, a couple of weeks before the autumn term began. All but two of the staff were male; the masters wore gowns for assembly and the ATC (Army Training Corps) ran around the playground on a Saturday morning (the English department rebelled, of course, with a poster on our office door reading 'Join the Army, See the World and Kill People'). I had no teacher training but tried to follow the advice of one colleague: 'Don't smile for the first term.' With the O-level group I plodded line by line through *Macbeth*, reproducing how I was taught English at my grammar school. Junior Latin was livelier. We followed the Cambridge course, using its bright orange pamphlets based on the everyday life of a family in Pompeii. Small boys quietly sniffled when Vesuvius erupted and 'Cerberus', the household dog, was ossified in ash for all time.

Did I ever intend to get married? While my fiancé took a fourth year at college, I acted like a parody of a working-class wife, buying fish fingers and frozen peas for our tea, picking up the dirty washing, taking it to the launderette, too tired for sex except at weekends. I used to bite my lip when I rang my mother from the public call box, keeping up the pretence everything was fine; I told myself that the miserable rows were signs of Lawrentian passion. Eventually some survival instinct kicked in, or else it dawned on me that this life was for real. I called the wedding off and moved out, flogging my engagement ring and a batch of LPs to clear the rent. My body reacted with cramping and vomiting; my hair thinned and my nails softened; an operation on my bowel was mooted. Not a moment too soon my mother, never a confident traveller, came post haste on buses all the way from Portsmouth to avert this. In my copy of Simone de Beauvoir's memoirs I underlined a passage, 'I would not sacrifice my autonomy to any man except to one who would not ask me to,' but being nursed back to health by my mother was hardly an auspicious beginning to adult life.

A series of stops and starts. I left teaching and took a room in a run-down Victorian terraced house near Clapham Junction, sharing with a friend from college and three others. In London I cleaned houses, modelled at Camberwell

Art College – clothes on – and then briefly followed a social worker around the high-rise flats on the Latchmere Estate in Battersea, writing a report for the National Association for Gifted Children (now Potential Plus UK). I interviewed boys and girls who were hyperactive and either highly articulate or nearly catatonic, all of them streets ahead at school; on Saturdays I ran a drama club for them and found my métier as a clown with a white face and a lipsticked wedge of smile.

What *was* I doing in my twenties? Like an anthropologist, I was learning the varieties of the English middle classes, fathoming their tribes, their diets, their native habitats and their ways of speech. I observed and experimented. I hoped, eventually, to pass as one of them. But they were legion! Fran, my closest friend from university days, came from Methodist farming stock who were teetotal. In their home, luxury and extravagance were frowned upon but they seemed to me to be very well off, living in a large manor house with several bedrooms and acres of land. The foreman, who came in at breakfast for a cup of tea and to discuss the day's work, was known by his first name, while her parents referred to themselves as 'Mr' and 'Mrs Bennett' in front of him as if in a Jane Austen novel. Fran bought all her clothes second-hand from Oxfam or market stalls. Yet Monica, the teacher with whom I shared a house near Bedford after my aborted wedding, wore her new clothes as soon as she bought them. I still kept clothes for 'best' and wore slippers in the house, but she pattered about on high heels, fully dressed and made up at breakfast. A scion of the Home Counties, she was an ardent cricket fan and listened to *The Archers*. Her parents donated a vast Edwardian suite for our lounge (not sitting room), covered in Sanderson cabbage-rose chintz. Monica and I sat in splendour downing gin and tonics together, feeling sophisticated.

Cleaning houses furnished me with further notes. The barristers in Clapham, for instance, who read *The Times*, chatted merrily with me or left friendly instructions with cake and chocolates. Their house off Northcliffe Road was a humble enough terrace but full of antique furniture, Turkish rugs and sherry decanters. I made 'real' coffee in a pot; their cooker was state of the art. On the other side of the Common, where I scrubbed the tidemark from the bath for a teacher and her children, the house was scruffy and chaotic. She wasn't used to servants, sat at the table smoking and nervously reading the *Guardian*, while I hoovered around her. Boyfriends refined my knowledge of caste distinctions. Peter's parents lived in a detached Beckenham home straight out of Osbert Lancaster or John Betjeman, a superior stockbroker-Tudor with parquet flooring and immaculate garden. His mother played professional tennis and gaily donned overalls to paint the kitchen, perching on a stepladder. Her family were, I believe, rather more upper middle than comfortable middle middle, but these were mysteries within mysteries. Peter's father, selling Jaguars for Dutton Forshaw in Mayfair, was surely a cut above David's. David's dad was also a businessman, working, more mundanely, for Shell: less cachet, though not necessarily less cash. David's mother, like Peter's, had also played at Wimbledon. A PE teacher from Birkenhead, she was one or two steps up from her proletarian past, forthright and funny, and a churchgoer. Sunday afternoon in the Surrey hills meant walking Crispin, the black Labrador, on the local

heath. Oh brave new world that had such people in it! And
they were all 'middle class'.

Boyfriends had long been my route into the world of
books, theatre and art. At school, they had saved me from
being freakish while the other girls sent me to Coventry and
tore down the pin-ups of George Best from the inside of my
desk. Boys never minded me being brainy. Yes, there was
snogging – Lawrence, when I was thirteen, who stuck his
tongue into my mouth to my horror, his own tasting musty
or mothballed (recklessly I vowed never to 'French kiss'
again); the hand creeping under the jumper to unlatch the
bra and the nerve-racking aim for the nipple, a sensation
I vainly tried to reproduce alone late at night in bed, suddenly pouncing on my own breast. There was dancing and
smooching – yes, all that – and listening to our LPs together,
and feeling an erection harden under grey serge school
trousers – yes, yes, all that – but always it was the talking that
I craved. The kissing and cuddling and holding hands, the
feeling each other and the fending off – all that was fine, just
fine, but the romance of another person and what went on
inside them, that was just as erotic.

In sixth form, Phil and I read Plato's *Republic* together and
debated the role of artists. As we listened to the Moody Blues,
Oscar Peterson or Alfred Brendel, we cut up the Sunday
Observer for our files on writers. We argued fiercely about
Lawrence's *Sons and Lovers*: were men *truly* different from
women? I thought not. I wasn't Miriam or Clara, I was Paul
Morel! – but he disagreed (Raphael, who liked the sound of
Phil, said I should have married him and he was probably
right). Now, in my twenties, the men in my life shared Lon-
don with me. All my spare cash went on theatre tickets or

exhibitions at the Tate, the Hayward and the Whitechapel; concerts at the Royal Festival Hall on the South Bank, or the Wigmore, tucked behind Oxford Circus. Peter had a car, a rarity then among twenty-somethings, a glamorous MG midget. We tried out Italian and French restaurants and then took a holiday 'abroad', driving across France and Spain with the MG's top down, me in a silk headscarf from Liberty's, the labyrinthine shop in Regent Street I had recently discovered, whose balconies were strewn like a bazaar with gorgeous carpets and fabrics.

Friends from Cambridge squatted or lived communally in Stoke Newington or Brixton and talked of crofts in Scoraig or Findhorn, but I had no desire to rough it. I liked feathering my nest with odds and ends I'd picked up in junk shops, a fruitwood Victorian mirror, a bamboo table. I moved into another shared house, a smart modern one, with wooden floors and Scandinavian-style Habitat furniture. Though I was cooped up in a dark box-room, the open-plan kitchen and the lounge on the upper level were bathed in light; floor-to-ceiling windows looked straight on to Wandsworth Common. We had a cleaning and shopping rota but were a disparate bunch: a gardener at Hyde Park who grew marijuana; a woman learning to be a tax inspector; and the landlady's son, who did not seem to do anything much. His mother, now resident in Earl's Court, was the widow of an English actor whose face I remembered from war films. I found a letter left casually lying around. 'How can you possibly bear,' the mother wrote to the son, 'to live with such *ordinary* people?'

★

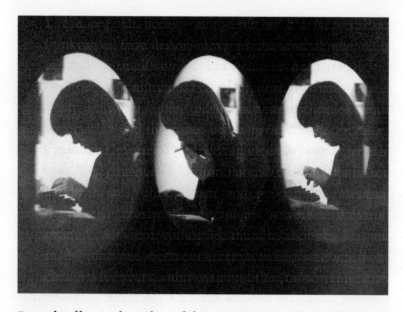

Periodically I thought of becoming a writer. There's a photograph of me taken by one of my housemates, Nigel, in the house near Clapham Junction. I am posing, aged twenty-two, in front of a borrowed typewriter, smoking a More's menthol cigarette (an affectation I soon gave up). I am probably writing poetry. I was a prolific poet from childhood; I had won prizes and seen my name in print; off to Cambridge, I was interviewed by the local paper as a juvenile celebrity so I was not lacking in self-regard. Yet the world of writing and publishing was utterly unknown territory: I had no passport. I knew no writers in person. They were fabled beings who taught and inspired and enhanced life. Since childhood I had also kept a journal and knew it to be a literary activity: 'The very act of putting pen to paper presupposes a certain detachment,' I wrote sagely at eighteen. But a diary was not 'art'.

Writing gradually insinuated itself into my life in my twenties and eventually took over. I have the women's movement to thank for that. Feminism, like writing, was a wedge, prising my life open. I was never any good at institutions, spoilt perhaps by being singled out at school, and far too shirty to take orders happily. At the BBC, training as a studio manager in radio, I was a restless subaltern who soon reached the limit of her technical competence. I bridled at the pep talks and tickings off from the crisply bloused personnel officer with a flutey voice like Joyce Grenfell, who reviewed our progress. I took umbrage when offhand, self-important producers in news programmes ignored me as I bent over a tape machine dishonestly removing the 'ums' and 'ahs' with a razor blade so that politicians might sound silver-tongued. Out of hours I joined a feminist writing group, then quite a novelty, run by the novelist Zoe Fairbairns, one of the Virago publishing 'collective', whose mesmerizing list of names appeared inside each volume from their press. My poetry was deemed 'too cerebral', so I read them brief opinion pieces on 'everyday sexism', as I called it, at the BBC. And I began a novel about three generations of women: my grandmother, mother and me.

No one with any ambition, I was told, stayed at the BBC's Bush House but would move elsewhere in the corporation, aiming ultimately for television. But the leisurely pace and the conviviality of the foreign language services at Bush were to my liking. One newsreader for the World Service wore a panama hat, as if suffering from the colonial heat, and brought a snifter with him to the studio, turning up insouciantly only seconds before I played in 'Lilliburlero' and the chimes of Big Ben. Night shifts were whiled away scribbling short articles for my women's group, eating nasi goreng in the canteen at 4 a.m., or flirting with the producers of the Persian service, whose erudition and worldliness were deeply seductive. I loved making the foreign language announcements. 'This is London calling,' I'd declare in mellifluous Hindi, or more brusquely in Polish. The Corporation encouraged us to apply for 'attachments' to other departments. Drama appealed to me, but on my first foray I had to stand up to my shoulders in a bin of magnetic tape waste for a play set in the jungle: 'Sound effects!' the director shouted at me impatiently. 'More rustle, MORE RUSTLE!' And I rustled. I rustled my way back to Bush House.

I was doing my best to settle down. With my boyfriend David, another BBC trainee, I rented a council flat in Walthamstow. We would have the 'right to buy' from the council, if we wanted, a move introduced by Mrs Thatcher, who was selling off social housing. The term 'yuppie' – 'young urban professional' – was coming into vogue. I was going to be one of them. I marvelled as the monthly sums in our joint building-society account book mounted, my first ever attempt at saving. A thousand each would be enough for a deposit on a terraced house. But my diary was full of warnings, Cassandra-like. I did not want to be a 'wife figure'; I did not want to be pregnant like all my friends, or disappear under the weight of childcare or my partner's moods and demands (though David did his own washing and ironing and was generally good-natured; he also typed all my pieces). I felt I was playing at houses and began to dread the future. 'I want to waste time again,' I wrote mournfully, adding 'how little I like the way society is arranged'.

Years later, when I confessed to Raphael that I voted for Mrs Thatcher in 1979, he said he was 'tickled' by it; amused, perhaps, by my naivety. Perhaps he saw it as a sign of my free spirit or perhaps, not brought up to admire the parliamentary parties, or think the Labour Party left-wing, he found it less momentous, looking back, than I did. I was young – twenty-four. Five years earlier, I had cast my first vote for Labour in keeping with an adolescence where I had seen nothing but red posters. Was I finally rebelling, cocking a snook at my parents, or did I just want to see a woman as prime minister, as though her being a woman would override every other consideration? This was one version of feminism that was all about 'empower-ment' or personal autonomy, and an ever-expanding notion of what women could do as equals – in business, in parlia-ment, wherever. It implied an endless self-expansion and a throwing off of social or sexual constraints.

Certainly I saw no contradiction a year or so later, attack-ing 'the Tories' in a handful of reviews for the feminist monthly *Spare Rib*. My articles were mostly indignant, rallying the troops. I had the breeziness of youth – the film-maker Bertolucci came under my hammer at one point for his sexual politics – and in my role as scourge I offered to write about popular television (there was no competition: no one else, Ruth Petrie, one of the editorial collective, told me, even admitted to watching it). I was cutting my teeth, gaining in confidence but also full of questions which my polemics could not answer. The new women's bookshops, Sisterwrite in Islington and Silver Moon in Charing Cross Road, overflowed with writing by women: fiction, poetry, essays, history, sociology and more from a bevy of independent presses such as Virago, the Women's Press, Sheba and Onlywomen. But what, if anything, made it *'women's* writing'? Writing by women did not spring up fully formed, like Athena from the head of Zeus. It was shaped by its time and place; it belonged to a specific culture. It had its sticking points too. What *did* I have in common with the other women in my writing group as we went on meeting and talking about our lives? With Manny, who was Iranian and had escaped the revolution; Mita, who was Czech and another escapee, though from Communism; Val, who broke taboos writing about postnatal depression; and Pauline, who had changed her name, become a lesbian and left her marriage and sons?

Again that need to step off the treadmill. At meetings of 'Women in the Media', a loose-knit group of older, professional women, I listened to their plans for changing television and radio production but knew I was not an activist. I did send an airy memo to the Assistant Head of Productions and Planning, suggesting a women's programme on contemporary politics for the World Service, and was politely fobbed off – 'they are human issues, not just female ones' – but I was too nervous to go and talk to him. Instead I wrote a short talk on *Testament of Youth*, Vera Brittain's memoir of her experiences during the First World War; it was broadcast on the World Service. Freelance work might be possible, I immediately imagined, though it was hardly a way to earn a living (*Spare Rib* paid a fiver for 900 words). Leaving the BBC was unheard of, but that added to the thrill of doing it.

One evening I huddled under the bridge by the Royal Festival Hall, pumping a telephone kiosk full of coins until I eventually ran out. The voice on the other end of the line was probing, energetic, funny and wonderfully *American*, hospitable to talk and to expounding ideas. Cora Kaplan was teaching at Sussex University. She had edited *Salt and Bitter and Good*, an anthology putting three centuries of poetry by women on the literary map, and *Aurora Leigh*, Elizabeth

Barrett Browning's epic in verse. I was startled to learn that the 'poetess' I knew only as languishing on a sofa in the film *The Barretts of Wimpole Street*, ringlets drooping, campaigned through her poetry for the abolition of slavery and for the reform of child labour, and that she had rivalled Tennyson as a candidate for the post of Poet Laureate. With a state grant for postgraduate work, I might study and write my novel at the same time. I could scent another breather ahead. Brighton would be my next port of call.

★

When Phil, my sixth-form boyfriend, had gone to read English at Sussex in 1972, I sneered at his writing an essay on the bicycle in Edwardian society and literature; now I wished I had read it. I wanted to understand the social impulse behind fiction, poetry and drama, how individual writers were part of that wider world which they reimagined, their writing part of history. Sussex was one of Britain's new universities set up in the 1960s to foster a more integrated approach within the Humanities. Learning was sociable and the atmosphere heady: seminars rather than tutorials, a plethora of reading groups across the disciplines, including a 'feminist forum', new journals, in which faculty and students were involved. Some of these, like Literature Teaching Politics, connected to a network of groups burgeoning across the country. In LTP meetings, and in the journal it produced, we argued about the limits of English as a subject, about education as a whole, about the idea of culture (I was very taken with the Italian Marxist Antonio Gramsci's idea of the 'organic' intellectual, who was not a special being, set apart from others, but emerged in every walk of life). I felt as if I was in the right place at the right time. But perhaps, unlike the girl I was at barely eighteen, I was simply old enough to make the most of my intellectual freedom.

Defying the ominous entries in my diary, I set up home again with David. Our savings of £2,000 and a mortgage for £17,000 bought us a two-up two-down terrace, its small backyard dominated by a giant feathery fennel. We painted the rooms buttermilk or magnolia, bought pine furniture as if it were a country cottage, and squeezed the huge chintz settee, kindly donated by Monica, my old schoolteacher friend, into the tiny sitting room. We got a cat. But the walls between private and public were continuing to dissolve. Stirred by hearing the left-winger Edward Thompson, full of fire like an Old Testament prophet, give a rousing speech for nuclear disarmament at an open-air meeting on Brighton's Level, we joined CND. We read Richard Mabey's *Food for Free*, discussed environmentalism, went vegetarian and talked about getting an allotment. David, now working in television, was commuting long hours; I was left to hang out in pubs and meet up with my new friends.

Suddenly, out of a cloudless sky, I was struck down by panic attacks, my heart racing, breathless, bent over double, then sobbing. Offered free psychotherapy by the university, I was frightened and highly suspicious, but also relieved. I thought it preposterous, this telling a stranger one's intimate thoughts and feelings. What if my parents found out and thought me 'mentally ill'? (I never told them.) I was proud, too, that I was 'doing' therapy like so many others I now encountered. I lambasted therapy to my therapist, its airlessness, its narrowly bourgeois version of family life; she took it all on the chin. In one session I related the misery of a recent holiday, spent with my parents and my sister's family in a gîte in the Dordogne. David had wisely lost his voice once we reached Calais. After a fruitless argument, my mother had laid into me: 'Why must you always give us a thesis on everything?' 'But that is what you are doing,' my therapist riposted, 'making a thesis of your life.' I felt buoyed up, as if language had become a raft.

This time, at least, there was no wedding to call off and David and I managed to stay friends. Eking out my postgraduate grant, I could just about handle a mortgage of £13,000 and buy a flat: 104 Albion Hill was financial ballast as well as a bolthole. 'My own front door!' I crowed in my journal. 'My own flat, which I could stay in till I die – if I can afford to pay the mortgage!' – affirming to myself, as diaries do, what I already knew. I set to painting the walls and saved my shillings for the electric meter. My parents saw it as a step back into spinsterhood, but I thought it an advance. I would be self-contained.

Oh, that image of my self upon the wall, bathed in sunlight! An apotheosis of sorts, of bliss in just being, of turning to one side of life and taking stock. Every day I sat in my diary as if it were the garden and gazed about me. I totted up my resources, listed my debts; I put my past in order, recapping and summarizing love affairs like a world-weary courtesan, and made plans for the future. At last I was mistress of my fate. I could look after myself. Later, in the first years of married life, I would return to this splendid vision of complete independence. I knew it to be a fantasy, but I mourned its loss all the same.

2   Falling

When I told a Brighton friend that Raphael had phoned me to talk about his work and that we were to meet, she assumed it was for dinner with others and I did not disabuse her. 'Oh,' she said off-puttingly, 'he has lots of romantic friendships with women.' I imagined a seraglio of bluestockings at his beck and call. He was, I noted in my diary, '"a famous social-ist"', the inverted commas implying a sophisticated distance from such things. Still, I was anxious that I wouldn't measure up and treated the forthcoming occasion rather as a PhD viva, though there was nothing to mug up on in advance.

I took the train to London and was there by six thirty, sit-ting outside the National Film Theatre on the South Bank of the Thames. Time passed. In the whirl of what must be a very busy life, he had surely forgotten. Stubbornly I waited and waited on my pine bench as my spirits sank. The August light was fading on the river; a folk singer strummed 'The Streets of London' or some other standard; the nearby trestle tables under Waterloo Bridge, with their piles of second-hand books, were slowly packed away. Suddenly Raphael rushed up, flustered and smiling. He had been waiting in the foyer. I hadn't checked inside, as if I half expected to be stood up.

Later this near-miss became part of the story we told each other, as lovers will, of our romance: how close to not meet-ing we came, the sheer fortuitousness of it. It was a happy fiction: we would surely have rung each other for an explanation; we were already in a reading group together, and would have met another time, and so on. In one of his love letters Raphael traced the 'what ifs' back *ad absurdum*: 'Supposing,' he concluded, 'they'd never built Portsmouth harbour, or your sixth-form English teacher had gone to another school?' All his anxieties, he wrote, were displaced on to the past. Nothing could go wrong between us in the future: 'All things are made anew.'

Lovers dramatize themselves as if they walk a tightrope across an abyss of contingency. They live in the time of miracles and not of the mundane; a time, not of history or chronology, but of revelation. With their sense of immanence they perceive the world aglow with goodness; their friends are angels. Falling in love is a mystery that only in retrospect becomes blindingly obvious: how could I not have fallen for him? I ask myself years later. But what makes us take that leap? To plunge headlong and risk immersion in another's element – to sink or swim? 'I fell for him,' we say in English, when what we mean is 'something pushed me': I was ready to fall.

It is the habit of narration also, moving ever forward but unable not to look back. The fabric of the past comes to us ready-made by the significance we later give to certain strands; and memory colludes like an elderly relative, telling the same story over and again. And, yes, the random livedness of a life escapes us; the messy, unfinished selvedge; the un-eventful, the unacknowledged. And all those other impressions, encounters, ideas, feelings, are sent back to the underworld to live in the shadows of our selves. And so I scatter asterisks like bright objects in my path which I must stoop to examine or pick out from the grass. I halt and reflect. I realize as I write that the person perched on the wall, in that image so dear to me, looking out to a distant sea, is also my ideal reader, poised on the edge of thought.

★

Before I fell in love with Raphael I spent four years living alone. Looking back I can see that Brighton was as much an education as the university. Brighton, with its pleasure dome and beach – London's sanatorium! – with its glamorous, gleaming crescents of white stucco, theatreland's home from home; sleazy Brighton, its hotels once the favoured rendez-vous for the dubious assignation and the dirty weekend, the wide boy and the co-respondent in his two-tone shoes; Brighton, which will always shimmer in my mind's eye as an oasis of self-love, while the disco music throbbed and small-town boys in exile danced their nights away, and the punkish girl bands strutted their stuff in clubs. Brighton, for homeopathy and yoga, for kidney beans, muesli and disgusting dandelion coffee from Infinity Foods, for the women who cropped their hair and put on lumberjack shirts; Brighton, a haven for a love that would reconfigure love, relationships from which you might float free. If the university gave me the ideas to think with and feminism laid me open to them, Brighton, dear, seedy, artful, self-advertising Brighton, offered me the space to play.

And play I did. I took my cue from new gay friends, especially the idea that a person need not fall in love with everyone they went to bed with; that desire could be sex without romance; that sex could be simply for pleasure, without guilt. Feminism, too, argued that there were many kinds of

intimacy and they need not conform to the hoary old plot of
courtship and seduction – the male as predator, the female as
prey – with a family as the goal. A 'relationship' was partial:
that was the point. It need not be merely frivolous either, a
'fling' or 'affair', pitting women against each other – the 'bit
on the side', 'the other woman', competing for male attention, jealous and possessive. Celibacy was another option,
especially for women, and not a failure. The choice need no
longer be between what Erica Jong once called 'the zipless
fuck', a casual encounter, or a cataclysmic merging of selves,
in which one partner was usually obliterated or subordinated.
I decided that I wanted to move in and out of people, without
'fuss and laceration', I wrote in my diary. Alternatively I
could retreat to bed in a grubby jumper and an old nightie,
away from the world and its 'sharp-pointed demands'.

So I experimented. I tried sleeping with a girlfriend (much
warmth and affection, some hilarity, but no lust); with male
colleagues (brief, often tender and always interesting); I tried
being in a triangle, or a quadrangle, and in my diary I ana-
lysed my feelings hot off the press:

When P. told me about sleeping with E., I felt first the rush of fear at
being hurt but it was hard beneath that to know if I actually was.
More the fear of rejection. And afterwards in the bath, I wanted,
almost, to dramatize, to explore a pain which actually wasn't there.
Instead a kind of queasiness, trying to keep my balance and steer my
way into new and difficult ways of relating. I have no models outside
monogamy. But I want to change, to test my reactions, to try growing new skin.

I wanted 'to unlabel'. I wanted 'no absolutes', not to be
defined by what I did in bed. I did not want a sexual 'identity',

or to wear it like a flag. I fell a little in love with everyone; but I held back. 'Perhaps one needs to be distant in order to love,' I wrote, putting my feelings at arm's length.

Of course my diary is hardly reliable. It isn't 'me'. It hides as much as it reveals and, like a memoir, it singles out my consciousness. I am insulated too from history while I stay wrapped up inside my personality. Comically earnest, pompous and sometimes endearing, the diarist trapped in those pages writes as if she comes fresh from the egg every day. The diarist is for ever young, even jejune, the plucky heroine of her life, the centre of a *Bildungsroman* that is evolving and will have – one day – a discernible plot. 'I' am, though, quite recognizable to myself, if only as a constant bystander, observing my life. For a while I had three diaries on the go. The daily journal; a work diary charting my reading, my freelance efforts and my debuts at conferences – speaking in public was nerve-racking but exhilarating ('always a Sarah Bernhardt,' my mother's ghost whispers); and a separate therapy diary describing my sessions. Was I hiding my ambitions and splitting off my emotions? Or giving them their due? My 'life' was surely more balanced than my diary (diaries). I might be living by my wits but I was also swimming, cycling, walking by the sea. The diary treated me as a project and the diary cheered me on.

My life was pretty quiet, not sensational or self-destructive. This was not an adolescent phase I was going through, nor a protest. I was twenty-eight, not eighteen. I had my own place and my own money. Plenty of sex; plenty of loneliness too, but I was also avoiding what was expected of me. Thanks to my diaphragm and condoms I never once became pregnant. All I had to contend with was the odd bout of cystitis and thrush (a garlic clove inserted in the vagina was soothing, though disconcertingly the fumes appeared on the breath), and one close shave with an STD, a red rash, itchy and sore, which had me queuing at the Brighton clinic and telling all my partners. AIDS was not yet on my horizon, though it soon would be.

For a time, until I had to earn a living again, I had no pattern to conform to or authority telling me what to do; I had no timetable either, unless I invented it. But I was part of a culture nonetheless. 'I am one of those people for whom safety is solitude,' I declared, but I was surrounded by friends with whom to share my experiments and in Brighton, lovely libertarian Brighton, my small neck of the woods, I would not be ostracized. My solitude was also shored up by the laws that had given women this relatively new freedom in British life. It depended on me renting or mortgaging under my own name and being left to live alone unmolested, on free and available contraception and the possibility of paid work. As a student I relied on a maintenance grant from the state for three years. The deposit for the flat came from profit made on the housing market, not from my own efforts. I might live as if self-directed by my will – which is how it appears in my diary and how we all must live – but I was a creature of my time and place. I thought I was special, as we all are, but I was also representative.

Two strands of thought, Marxism and psychoanalysis, slowly undermined the idea of a sovereign self, of my being simply free to make my life as I saw fit. The first argued that we were not simply agents of our lives but that our lives were limited by social and economic forces outside ourselves; the second that we can never know 'our selves' but remain subject to uncontrollable drives, unconscious motivations, inhibitions and cravings. We were also made by all those 'invisible presences', as Virginia Woolf called them, which live inside us and fashion our sense of who we are. When I encountered Woolf's memoirs, I was struck by her image of the difficulty she found in writing of the relation between an individual and those larger forces that shape us. 'I see myself as a fish in a stream,' she wrote, 'deflected; held in place; but cannot describe the stream.' Much of what I read back then proposed that the division was part of the problem: the self was never still, always being formed. We *are* the stream as well as the fish that swim in it.

If I was becoming an oddball by the standards of my upbringing, I should not claim too much. I never became a bohemian, liking my comforts far too much (I applied for a council grant for repairs to the flat and, after being half poisoned by the smelly Calor gas fire, for two new night storage heaters). I was never much of a communitarian, being far too interested in my own development. Not coming from the middle classes I had little instinctive conventionality – Raphael soon challenged what was there – but equally little need to rebel against it. My politics were largely untheorized, if deeply felt: an inherited sense of social injustice and an innate sympathy with the have-nots; a belief in what D. H. Lawrence called 'life values' as opposed to 'money values'. I was in search of a shared philosophy of life, much as I had been when I read Blake or Cicero or Marx in my sixth form, or when, a thirteen-year-old hippy disguised by school uniform, I hid my cowbell in my desk, or lay on my bed at home murmuring the refrain from 'Woodstock': '*We are stardust, we are golden, And we've got to get ourselves back to the garden.*'

Invisible presences. Before I went to college at eighteen, my father, with a tinge of melancholy, said to me, 'I expect you'll be sitting up all night, putting the world to rights.' He was a man of philosophical bent who kept tags of poetry in his wallet, and with him I sat mulling over the meaning of life, man's inhumanity to man, and the 'fourth dimension', as he called it. My mother, far less speculative, made no show of my leaving. She was fond of a passage from *The Prophet* by Kahlil Gibran, one of my teenage inspirations, where children were deemed 'living arrows' whom mothers let fly: 'Your children are not your children . . . they come through you but not from you.' She did not want to hold me back, and I admire her for that. Ten years later, though, I was going a bit too far afield; their daughter was a kind of prodigal who might one day return home. They were waiting for me to grow out of my funny ideas.

Those two bags of groceries I remember carrying up the steep incline of Albion Hill – what are they if not full of the past? I wanted to take my parents with me; I was eager to see them. My father was slightly mystified by the flat, while my mother was excited; the dream of independence appealed to her, as it would to many women. But I finally had a private life outside the pattern of the family and I kept secrets: my mother once aptly accused me of being 'arsey', literally retentive. No wonder that my novel was stymied. I was too close to the lives of my mother and grandmother, afraid of turning them into colourful, garrulous 'characters' or objects of pathos, standard roles for working women in fiction. I could no more imagine simply shuffling off the past than I could find a way of writing about it.

Soon enough the money was running out and my doctorate was also in limbo. Instead of focusing on its official topic,

I read popular fiction on the side as if I were still a girl, bunking off from lessons. I was permanently broke, regularly borrowing small sums from friends. Scholarly articles gave me kudos but not cash. I took on short part-time courses for bossy, knowledgeable students at the Workers' Educational Association and the rather better-heeled in Sussex villages at the Open University, and then applied for a job in the Humanities Department of Brighton Poly. Working with historians, art historians, philosophers and geographers, designing a degree that crossed the disciplines, suited me down to the ground. A senior colleague, though, thought I asked too many questions about our set texts in English, which had not changed for years; another thought me far too full of myself, brimming with 'Cambridge' arrogance.

At the poly it was brought home to me again that teaching was not a matter of simply passing on knowledge but of getting people to think for themselves; that education was about creating a better common culture and that a system which promoted a few people up the social ladder, leaving the rest behind, resentful and undervalued, was hardly worth the candle. My parents, who were thought 'uneducated', had long ago taught me that education and intelligence were not the same thing. So much to discuss, but I was working frenetically hard. If only, my diary sighed, I could bring the compartments of my life together! If Raphael hadn't existed, I would have needed to invent him.

★

Romance was much on my mind. Literally. I had been thinking about it hard and published my first scholarly article, off my own bat, a piece on Daphne du Maurier's *Rebecca*. It was fuelled by an old-fashioned indignation. I was furious at the Marxist critics I was encountering who called romance readers 'dupes' and saw their longings as a kind of 'false consciousness'. Romance, I argued, not quite pontificating, was always a sign of restlessness and discontent; of wanting more than was on offer. All those 'true love' stories I had devoured as a girl, doctors and nurses gazing into each other's eyes, all those mass-market romances, might be, like religion, 'the opium of the people'. But they were, as Marx also wrote, 'the heart of a heartless world'.

A History Workshop at Ruskin College in Oxford on 'Popular Romance from Robin Hood to Mills & Boon' was right up my street. Conference-going was new to me. Most were far less professionalized than they are now, but History Workshops were in a class of their own. I'd had a taste of their ecumenical approach, venturing briefly to a 'Religion and Society' event held at the huge Friends House on the Euston Road. The place was teeming and the atmosphere purposeful yet festive, a cross between a mass meeting and a scholarly jamboree. 'Tickets limited to 700,' the poster announced cheerfully; there was wheelchair access and a crèche; fees were minimal – 'Students, OAPs and the unwaged' paid next to nothing – and the workshop, running from Friday to Sunday each day from 10.30 a.m. to 6 p.m., involved over 140 speakers in panels ranging across countries, periods and topics, both narrowly focused and broad-brush. My friend Alex from Sussex, working on women's central role in spiritualism, was one of the speakers, but I felt out of place among historians.

The one-day symposium at Ruskin College was much lower-key, though the main hall was packed. Someone pointed Raphael out to me as the *genius loci*. Sitting on the floor with his arms around his knees, during the closing session he looked like the 'Eternal Student' in his bomber jacket, scruffy jeans and 'granny' glasses, long hair flopping over his eyes as he smoked a roll-up. 'A bit of an old hippy,' I thought, mistaking him for the generation of 1968. Six months later we came face-to-face at London's Institute of Contemporary Arts. A chic, all-but-subterranean gallery and cinema, its entrance in The Mall, it was incongruously tucked into the rear of the grand cream-coloured façade of Carlton House. The ICA was Ruskin's polar opposite, hosting unashamedly highbrow or avant-garde talks, exhibitions and screenings, but there was Raphael, giving a talk, and Cora, my doctoral supervisor but fast becoming a friend, introduced me to him in the queue for coffee. Memory supplies him with an improbable beret, though it is more likely a mnemonic for that day's theme – 'Crossing the Channel' – exploring the influence of ideas from France on British culture.

Raphael asked me a series of gentle, courteous questions about myself and appeared spellbound by my answers, utterly concentrated on our exchange. I was immediately seduced by his attentiveness. In those few minutes I felt special, singled out by someone whose learning clearly far outstripped mine but who did not feel the need to display it. In the years to come I was to see many times how powerful the spotlight of his attention was and how disappointed, even resentful, others could be when this focus faltered or moved on. But there was no *coup de foudre*. Impossible, anyway, to remember that look from those dark brown eyes. His face is so illuminated by our later love, its radiance obscures any detail. I think I thought him dishy; it was, I thought, a very Jewish face (though I was to be angry with my mother when she suggested this) – intense, reflective and kind. Yet the scene captures something of what was so charismatic in Raphael, a rare capacity to listen. And I wanted so much – who doesn't? – to be heard.

Unbidden, two childhood pin-ups float into my mind out of the ether of memory. First, an image of a mildly Semitic Jesus praying in the garden of Gethsemane, a poster of a sickly Victorian painting given to me at Sunday School, which I put over my bed for a while; and the other, an image of Ruster, the beloved Alsatian dog, on whose neck I hung whenever we visited my father's brother and his wife. What are they doing here, these banal phantoms, intruding on my reverie? Are they simply born of an urge to debunk and deflate? Both solemnly evoke a lustrous, soulful gaze and an infallible devotion beyond the merely human. Lovers – and we were no different – spend hours gazing into each other's eyes.

Not long after meeting Raphael, I joined the popular fiction reading group which had convened the Ruskin event. Sitting in his kitchen, where the group met once every month or so, I realized I had never known anyone so galvanized by talk, so full of exuberant energy. His entire body was involved in speaking as he leant across the table, his sentences accelerating, his hands raised for emphasis or his palms spread wide, a shrug or his index finger across his mouth when he paused for thought, as if stopping the flow. He seemed lit up from within by the sheer pleasure of thinking and arguing. Did people really strike their foreheads with their palms as he did? I found it delightful and theatrical, watching him hunch over the cup cradled in his hands, as if protecting himself from a Siberian wind blowing through Spitalfields. The coffee,

hissing and spluttering in the screw-top moka pot on the back
burner, was bitter and viscous, and as foreign as the gesticula-
tion. But it was the real thing.

I had seen Raphael's name on the spine of a book – *People's
History and Socialist Theory* – and picked up the gist of a recent
controversy among historians and others. A more positive,
even heroic notion of 'the people', as shaping their own
culture, history and class consciousness, was at odds with
thinking more broadly about 'popular culture' as that which
the majority of people read or enjoyed but which might be
fashioned for them. Hence the current critique of romance
fiction: popular but hardly radical. In 1984, though, the idea
of studying popular fiction, let alone teaching it, was a star-
tling one. The group interpreted 'popular' generously. We
chose books which fell into the obvious categories of 'genre',
such as nineteenth-century sensation novels or detective fiction, but also those which prompted particular ways of seeing
the popular or 'the people', or stimulated new kinds of reader-
ship and new forms of reading. Our discussions fed into many
future projects, individual and collective.

So I sat in Raphael's kitchen for eighteen months or so, as
we read our way through 'Criminal Cities' and 'Autobiography', cut wedges from a dozen clocks of Brie, munched
baskets of crackers, downed scores of bottles of wine. I must
have looked at his face a thousand times but somehow I did
not see it. Not as a lover would. Only when he became in
some way recognizable to me, and within, as it were, my
reach, could there be love 'at first sight'. Both of us were
'involved', as they say, with other people, so I don't suppose
he 'saw' me much either. And yet these other relationships
did not stop us later. By then he had become a person and not

simply, as he first appeared to me, an eccentric in his old curiosity shop of a house. By then I knew that others were half in love with him, affectionate towards him in meetings, hinting at lingering intimacies. But if I ever thought about Raphael as a potential partner, I never admitted it to myself. Or, at least, not to my diary.

★

There seemed no reason why living alone should not go on indefinitely: writing, teaching, occasional lovers. A good life, indeed a privileged one, but spent on a plateau of sorts. Occasionally I thought about having a child, but it was notional, a way of imagining a future. What if I shared with a woman friend? Another experiment. It would be fun, and different, and good for me too, I thought, before I got too used to my own company. I started looking at houses with my friend Sue, who could supply another salary and I the cash for a deposit when I sold my flat. Then Raphael rang me for a tête-à-tête.

In a file called 'Country Look', containing notes pasted on to pink paper headed 'Neo-Vict paint ranges', with 'Alison Light' at the top, he kept a record of our first telephone conversation. He was writing about 'neo-Victoriana' and, in particular, 'retrofitting', the periodizing of houses that was part of the new 'Do It Yourself'. Had I ever perhaps been to the home-improvement mega-stores like B&Q or MFI? (I had.) Did they sell plastic cornices and ceiling roses, dado rails or maybe fake wrought iron? (They did.) Could we meet to talk about it? (We could.) We set a date.

On the phone we had talked for an hour but this was how he worked, smoking and writing while he listened (pause – a deep drag on the cigarette; scuffling sounds with paper). I scribbled him a postscript later that night (also in the file). Did he know that a whole section of kitchenware now had a Victorian slant: weights and scales, pine salt boxes, skillets, enamel utensils, spice racks? But how did Raphael intuit that I knew about such matters? Had I talked about decorating my Brighton flat and painting its walls 'apple-blossom' ('white with a hint of green', as it said on the tin) or one of the other 'country whites'?

That first evening when we met outside the NFT on the banks of the Thames, we began with argument. I was still smarting from a weekend with a boisterous six-year-old who kept thumping me round the head with his metal toy; his parents reasoned with him and left him to it. I thought a smack might be effective; Raphael saw all forms of corporal punishment as child abuse. Then we disagreed about class. Had class distinctions been worse at Balliol in the 1950s than at Cambridge in the mid 1970s? Surely so, said Raphael, remembering young 'gentlemen' in velvet smoking jackets with their braying voices, their sense of entitlement, and the cult of the Oxford man with his 'first-rate mind'. 'You are living evidence,' he insisted, of how much the 'ancient' universities had changed. He was right. And yet so was I. 'Class' was a volatile matter of feeling for me, of a corrosive, shameful sense of inferiority, belligerence, envy and pure hatred, not a uniting force for solidarity. Teaching at Ruskin, Raphael daily came across adult students who were often deeply unconfident beneath their bold exteriors, crippled by these feelings. But he had never felt them.

On we went, sharing our life histories, to a Chinese restaurant in Soho, where Raphael told me about his mother,

Minna, calling her by her first name and explaining that she was a composer. She had been only one of his mothers, he explained. His aunties, Miriam and Sarah, and a close family friend, Ray (short for Rachel? I wondered), had all provided homes for him after his parents' marriage broke up. His mother now lived with her second husband in Buckinghamshire, but his father, Barnett, was dead. Minna's politics, he said, had torn the marriage apart. I had never heard anyone talk, as he did, about being 'brought up' a Communist, as one might a Catholic or a Muslim.

It had all been so easy: 'He never intimidates,' I wrote in my diary, as if I expected to be. 'I like being put into a taxi on Westminster Bridge,' I added, aware of the novelty of letting myself be looked after. I could accept Raphael's attentions since he was impeccably well-mannered with everyone. 'It was presumptuous,' I wrote, slightly unctuously, to imagine more than friendship. I was protecting myself, as lovers do, against getting my hopes up – but why write it down if imagination was not already stirring? A week later, and another meeting, the ground was shifting: 'It might be possible to fall in love with him,' I reckoned, 'despite the impossible hair!'

Margarethe von Trotta's *Rosa Luxemburg* at the Lumiere in St Martin's Lane was not much of a date movie, with its bleak and terrible execution scene and the dumping of her body, like the socialist future, into the depths of a canal. We held hands briefly and, as we walked back to his house across Holborn Viaduct and towards St Paul's, Raphael put his arm round my shoulder. Again I refused to read anything into it and told myself, 'This is probably what he does with "comrades".' A spontaneous embrace led to a chaste, slightly stunned night together on the lumpy futon he offered to guests. Waking to find him gone downstairs to the kitchen, I thought that perhaps he always spent the night with his women friends. Raphael's lodger, a beautiful medievalist working on religious communities, joined us for breakfast and that threw me further. Virginia lived in the attic. For all I knew she also shared his bed. Was I imagining a left-wing Lothario? Possibly. I was out of my depth.

With perfect timing, Raphael was in Brighton two days later, speaking at a fringe event for the Trades Union Congress, an unlikely setting for a romantic tryst. Across the road from the Old Ship Hotel we lay on the pebble beach in the dark; next morning my short blue coat was covered in tar. All lovers fall in love the same way: the rapture of discovery; the nights of talk and love-making; the exhaustion and the ecstatic dwelling on the other's image, taking it all in. On the train back to London after that first night, Raphael wrote immediately to say that he was shivering and that these 'unidentifiable tremors' could only mean that 'something must have happened between us'. My note crossed with his as if we were still in the same room.

It was a glorious autumn. We went blackberrying in the sun on the Sussex Downs; dancing in pubs; and we met under the railway clock at Brighton station, which became our lodestar, the sign of joyous reunions. We stood in Spitalfields market at two in the morning, haggling over trays of fruit with the wholesalers, the sacks of leeks and potatoes gleaming in the moonlight. And we started writing together, a review of *Rosa Luxemburg*, and that was bliss too, puzzling over the film's intention, and whether a biopic, however sophisticated, with its emphasis on an exceptional individual, could ever convey the collective politics of a socialist movement. Heaven, very heaven.

According to Raphael we were 'courting', a deliberate archaism in the face of our modern lives. We both stopped 'seeing' other people. He didn't want a 'relationship', he said; nor would he be my 'partner', as if we were setting up a firm of solicitors together. All or nothing. I agreed. After a couple of weeks he proposed to me. Was it in the Commercial Tavern, a shabby Victorian hostelry with plush wallpaper and velvet chairs? I don't recall, but I remember the little shrug and the slight moue he made, almost a parody of a Jewish comedian, and the hint of a suggestion as he ventured to say, 'If we go on getting along as well as this, darling, perhaps we might get married' – less a question than a statement of the obvious. The wedding was nine months later. A whirlwind romance, but what are months, weeks or minutes to new lovers? Feeble scratches on the wall of time. We had flown the coop. We were soaring in mid-air.

3   Courting

A love story always begins in the middle. A person is a crowd as well as an individual and comes not only with a history but with a thickly wooded present and a future lit by hopes and desires. The exclusivity of falling in love and the blithe exhibitionism that usually accompanies it – 'Look at us! Look at us!' – do not often last, unless they are the basis of the relationship, two peacocks preening, and not simply one of its modes. The world comes in: workmates, friends, family, old flames, to make more elastic that initial bond. We call a lack of give 'possessiveness'. Like mourning, love is meant to go through its stages, relinquishing that first life-saving hold on each other, the relief of rescue, and the laying of sole claim. That's not quite how it was with us.

Raphael was 'Raph' when I met him. He was everybody's property; he could be phoned or called on at his home at any time (dropping in to use his lavatory was not unheard of). Comrades from across the world would turn up at short notice, expecting a bed or a floor, a meal and a conversation that went on half the night. 'Another twelve Italian Marxists for breakfast!' I would joke, or half joke – he had once entertained such a group and wowed them with sausage, bacon and fried eggs. God's motley came and went: elderly Party members and fellow travellers; those who belonged to – the distinctions had to be mastered – the 'old' New Left and 'new' New Left from the late 1950s and the 1970s respectively; anarchists, Trotskyites,

Eurocommunists, militants and contrarians; all manner of trade unionists, railway men and miners, and Labour politicians, many of whom were or had been students of Ruskin; local East End villains, whose life stories Raphael was busily recording; sophisticated French scholars of memory bearing silk scarves from Paris; American and Australian leftists; postmodernists and eager postgraduates from all over; publishers, writers, journalists, conservationists, museum workers, archivists, teachers, the History Workshop editorial collective and old Workshop hands; dear friends, old lovers, extended family and friends of family – many with lives and histories interwined.

Brought up from a very young age to privilege the life of the group over that of the individual, Raphael was 'allergic', he told me, to the idea of the self, finding it distasteful, or at least not wholly credible. I was often baffled when he talked of 'we': 'we have decided to' or 'we were looking at', he'd say, speaking, not of us but of Ruskin College or History Workshop or some other collectivity, infinitely preferring identity with others to the first-person pronoun. His 'Communist unconscious', he said, preferred to translate 'I want' – the mantra of possessive individualism – into the impersonal.

My ego had a different history. With my new-found independence and my beginnings as a writer, I took my 'self' rather seriously and yet it, if it was an 'it', felt infinitely porous and unsure. Raphael once suggested affectionately that in Marxist terms our marriage would be 'a dialectical union of opposites'. From two very different people, something new, a third entity – 'the marriage' – would be made. How the process would come about – the transformation – was left obscure. It sounded rational and painless.

★

A few lines from Raphael, written late at night and not long
after we met, began:

Dear Love,

Further to my previous note, for God's sake, don't buy any
vegetables. I have the two big aubergines we bought on Sunday, the fat cauliflower, the half pound of mushrooms, a giant
beetroot, a bag of fresh herbs, two baby marrows, and sundry
greens . . .

Raphael was proud of my vegetarianism, but this succulent
inventory – a 'fat' cauliflower, 'giant' beetroot, 'sundry
greens' – and the urgent imperative were seductively literary.
The way to my heart was also through words; from the first
he had offered me a room and a desk to work at in Elder
Street. Now, lest the thought of a vegetable-eating marathon
was off-putting – though we might, he also inevitably suggested, make a meal for 'one or two' others – he ended with a
deliberate flourish. Come the weekend, he wrote, given his
'present uncomfortable physical state', which was seriously
disturbing his evening's work, 'I don't want to lose an hour's
fucking'. 'I adore you for that as for all your other gifts,' he
added extravagantly: who could resist such an invitation to
this feast of pleasures?

Raphael's letters were a storm of energy. At first they were
bulging with a list of unavoidable obligations which he was
only too happy to share if I managed to visit midweek. Would
I care to accompany him and Guy, a fellow History Workshop editor, to interview Arthur Scargill, the controversial

miners' leader, about anti-nuclear campaigning for a pamphlet 'we are getting up' for the Labour Party, 'trying to lift the encirclement on the miners'? Or have dinner with the editor of the *New Statesman* and a few members of the History Workshop collective who would be dropping by? (I bowed out of both.) A 'free' day held only two or three appointments, though there was always a deadline or two snapping at his heels or a crisis at Ruskin, where he taught. When Ruskin students boycotted a lecturer, David Selbourne, for writing for *The Times* while the Wapping printworkers were on strike (these were adult students, most of them trade unionists), Raphael worked all night to reply to Selbourne in the press, took a three-hour nap, and then started another article. I was both exhilarated by the public nature of his life and daunted. He thought me equal to anything.

Initially Raphael's letters to me were typed, but with so many corrections, additions and deletions that they looked like manuscripts. Then, quite soon, as we spent more time together, his listing of pressures fell away and he wrote by hand and almost entirely of love, experimenting, as it were, with personal feelings, though he was always more comfortable writing of himself in the passive tense. I ticked him off for using 'fucking' – a bourgeois swearword, I thought, in his case, full of unnecessary bravado. He needed to practise, he replied, writing about the body; he loved how we had resuscitated playground terms in our speech – 'dawdle', 'cheeky' – though he had never heard of 'the French kiss'. It was as though he was writing his way into an interior. Food and domestic matters were woven into our endearments – my hunting for a new washer for his coffee pot became a running theme. He was learning, he said, English habits: 'I want to add Sunday afternoon tea to our narrative, not perhaps its most passionate passages, but for me at least a reassuring one and also a novelty'; he would learn to toast crumpets. Like all lovers we made a history of 'our' story. 'What's the next stage in the construction of this narrative,' wrote Raphael, briefly sporting the language of literary theory, 'realism or fantasy?'

My letters, on the other hand, were rarely witty and rarely edited. I wrote disquisitions about my feelings, with no holds barred; I wrote about the cuts to education at the poly; about what I had dreamt the night before (he took to doing that too); about the problems of writing; about friendship; about teaching; about chores; about the sea and the weather. Nothing fazed him. I could never think too much, talk too much or feel too much for Raphael. And I was so *interested* in him, knew that I would never know him – too many years, too much unshared history. I felt it freed me. I would never be bored. It was also irresistible to let myself be tenderly looked after, and a satisfying turnaround for Raphael. He was often seen as helpless – 'You've got your work cut out,' one of his friends said to me early on – but Raphael enjoyed being my caretaker and 'a consort', bringing me snacks of figs and rum, or pears and Stilton, on a tray while I sat working. I let him buy me a jacket at Liberty's, though if he had been a younger man I might have run a mile. I loved being an object of desire.

All barriers were down and I was letting the world in, letting Raphael in, at an unconscionable rate. In counterpoint to the speed of the courtship, my diary mulled over the days at a snail's pace. With Raphael I threw caution to the winds, but the diarist was a judicious, sensible person. Occasionally my letters expressed my fears – the reader can imagine them all too easily. I caught colds and fevers; my digestive troubles returned, with cramping and vomiting. I took myself to bed. This was a pattern that repeated throughout our married life. Raphael had more stamina than me, both physically and mentally. I felt more alive with him and I felt exhausted often too. I often felt 'beside myself' with feeling.

I'm not sure that he ever understood my anxiety that I would be overwhelmed by his commitments or the sheer pace of his life. He simply breezed through my fears, brushing them away like cobwebs. He had no doubts and I was bowled over by his absolute faith in me. Our being together, he thought, exceeded all the bounds of his 'normally restricted emotional economy'. It was 'the world turned upside down' : 'A huge revolution in my imaginative life,' he added, 'not to think of sleep and bed as things to fight.' It was the principle of hope, in binary opposition to all the negativities in life, including the political climate (Mrs Thatcher's heyday). He revelled in our romance's 'pleasures of inversion' – the differences of culture, temperament, age. Now he could immediately give up smoking and maybe love would also miraculously free up his writing, a crabbed output, which proceeded, he said, 'by paralysis'. When his dear friend Gareth gently suggested that he might read Stendhal's *L'Amour*, Raphael knew he was being teased but thought we should get a copy nonetheless: 'It's not likely to be among the Labour History section of the library at Ruskin.'

What did he see in me? Can I answer that without being coy or making the reader wince? Probably not. Of course he thought I was wonderful in myself. What else? I came with a relatively blank page. I had not slept with any of his comrades, knew nothing of old political betrayals or loyalties or the complicated history of semi-incestuous moves between collective members. I came from the working classes but my world was not that of organized labour. Too young to be a disillusioned vanguardist or a jaded Marxist intellectual, like him I was sympathetic to the generation of 1968, though not of it. Raphael was grateful too that I was not Jewish and liable to claim kinship; his feelings were complicated on that score. I was eager and open and not afraid to argue; my mind, if not unmoulded, was not yet set. I was, he wrote – and this was another happy fancy – 'a child of nature' where he was 'wooden' and mechanical. I loved my garden and animals, enjoyed sex, and sang in the bath. And I made him laugh. But I believed him too, as the letters dwindled and the time together expanded, the days spent alone turned into weekends away, the weekends to a week in Brittany that was a liberation from my family's Christmas, and then, after a fortnight's Easter break spent between our homes, with room for tension and time to recover, he wrote 'with astonishment' not only of our deepening sense of love but of 'a quite new experience', 'inner peace'. 'Please God we get ten years,' Raphael said, though he didn't believe in Him.

*

On an early theatre trip we saw the recent revival of the hit musical *Me and My Girl*, the show that launched the dance craze of the Lambeth Walk in the late 1930s. Looking back at the original script, we were struck by how the new version was more conservative, seeming to approve the gentrification of the working classes rather than simply celebrating them as the heart of the nation. Our co-written review in the Christmas edition of *New Society* publicized our romance. We wanted to show each other off and naturally assumed that others would be as taken as we were with the new constellation of our lives. Inevitably, too, I found myself cold-shouldered, subject to sullen looks and some unguarded comments ('You look healthy,' a female friend of Raphael's told me on first meeting, as if assessing my childbearing capacity). I was not a model or a blonde beauty but youth is itself a trophy, seen as rejuvenating for the older man: 'His last chance for a young woman,' another remarked.

I knew that Raphael was also a prize, the older, more powerful man – had I not identified with tomboy Jo in *Little Women* when she finally found her professor? To some, Raphael's falling in love with a younger woman seemed banal and predictable, and not to be taken entirely seriously; it was a cliché, after all. But the longer the romance went on, the more it might seem as if he were abandoning his friends. Friendship – comradeship would have been Raphael's word – was an absolute good and at the centre of Raphael's life. Socialism exalted the collective, but I was in love with an individual.

The twenty-year gap between us unsettled peer groups and crossed the generations. That was part of the attraction for us both. It liberated us both from convention – so we thought – and allowed us to be singular. Marrying an older man also kept *me* young; at thirty I was often, among Raphael's friends, the youngest person in the room, as I had been the youngest in the family. I was used to seeing myself as precocious. I was sometimes jealous or resentful of his long-standing intimacies, but in those early heady days, firmly in the spotlight of Raphael's attention, it mattered little. The differences between us were stimulants, sources of wonder not distress.

Except. My parents had never heard of Raphael or his work and in their world he was a bizarre choice for a potential son-in-law. We swept down on them barely a month after meeting, basking in mutual admiration. Off we went on the customary stroll along the seafront while the roast cooked: Raphael and my father ahead, my mother muttering at my side. Raphael was their generation, only two years younger than my mother, but he was the last sort of man she would have chosen: a 'weirdo', political, skinny and scruffy. And he was Jewish. 'Where was he born?' was almost her first question, when I telephoned to say I'd met someone new called Raphael (I could not bring myself to call him a boyfriend). 'London,' I replied, deliberately obtuse. 'That's not an English name,' she countered. No matter that Raphael was not interested in his Jewishness, he *looked* so stereotypically Semitic. 'Is he circumcised?' she asked me, as we looked out to the Solent. I refused to answer.

That day he cut a particularly odd figure. In his haste he had grabbed unmatched suede boots short-sightedly from the bottom of a cupboard, one pale blue, one grey, while his spectacles, having come a cropper in one of our embraces, were held together with sticking plaster. Raphael fell into my father's category of 'egghead' or 'absent-minded professor' – not a threat or likely to knock him off his perch. Dad, in his turn, was instantly recognizable to Raphael, who was used to working men, and they soon found congenial talk. My mum, though, took a dim view of this suitor. She cast me as an innocent girl mesmerized and seduced by a Svengali. Instinctively she knew that Raphael's difference was part of the attraction; the strength of her reaction registered this. In choosing him, I was moving further away from where I came from. I was jumping the generations too, and in this there was a kind of triumph, as if I was saying, 'I am your equal.'

After Sunday dinner her grilling of him was worthy of Lady Bracknell. Raphael failed on all counts. He had a house, it was true, but he couldn't drive (neither could I, but that was irrelevant) and, he announced proudly, he *never* took holidays. My parents, hard at work from their teens, and at last able to afford holidays abroad, found Raphael's admission worrying – how did he relax? – and it also robbed them of a neutral area for conversation. That he was a teacher, they both respected – but at a trade-union college, neither school nor university, an anomaly in the British education system? An obvious 'lefty', he had never been married and did not have children – not a good sign; he was not a family man. Nor was he my mother's idea of a Romeo. While my father still bore a resemblance to Clark Gable, Raphael was bald on top, with a slick of hair wrapped across his forehead, and a wiry, rather than a muscular, frame. My mother would have been amazed to learn that in certain circles he was considered quite a catch.

Raphael was equally shocked by her. When he praised my work to her, she shot him down in flames. She couldn't see the point, she said, of writing about rubbishy authors like du Maurier. He did not then understand her inverted snobbery (she would never have watched *Coronation Street* or any other soap opera that was deliberately aimed at her class) or the frustrated intelligence which made her so defensive. I explained to Raphael that fury was what drove her on. It fuelled the energy that had got her family out of the gutter, saved my father from his melancholy moods and enabled her to stand her ground in the marriage. She always came out of her corner with her gloves on and fists up. Still, it was immensely relieving for me to have Raphael as a shield.

After we left, a family crisis was declared and my sister scooted down to Portsmouth on the pretext of my father's birthday. The Portsmouth equivalent of E. M. Forster's 'telegrams and anger' ensued – endless phone calls, in which Sandra acted as a broker, and my mother passed on the message through her that it wasn't *him*, it was 'the age thing'. She could not bear to think of all the years that would be 'lost' on widowhood and she was 'disappointed' in me. I felt winded – and wounded too by her anti-Semitism, which I did not broach.

Raphael decided to intervene. He wrote to my mother, thanking her for lunch and them both for the hospitality. Sincerely meant, it was also a playful, literary letter and highly polished (with the usual crossings out). He wrote that he understood her misgivings about him and, like all good rhetoricians, he repeated the charges against him, especially that he was 'miles older than Alison', painting a picture of my wheeling him about in his bath chair, which was hardly reassuring. He was not English but was passionately attached to English history, despite being brought up to be against war and suspicious of armies and navies; he did not have a sense of humour, he claimed – yet the whole letter was skittish and whimsical. 'I am quite a good cook' was a point he made in his defence, 'and enjoy seeing Alison well fed', a strange way of putting it, usurping my mother's place. 'As well as being lovers,' he added, a phrase quite alien to my mother's ears, we were 'very good friends' who worked well together. He enclosed the piece we had written on *Me and My Girl* as evidence – what, I wondered, would my mother make of that? Surely our 'otherness' was not wholly a bad thing? he finally asked. The age difference could actually be an advantage. It meant treasuring each moment, 'because it's all there is for certain'. So many of the most devoted couples, he finished, had a kind of 'deadness' in their lives together.

It was a touching letter, if somewhat wrong-headed, and my mother thought it funny and 'charming'. She told me she felt sorry for the 'poor bloke', having to write it at all. I also penned a missive, full of love for them and for Raphael, and urging them to trust me. Finally my mother answered, making peace. 'As a mum I can only say that you are Alison and I cannot think of anything that you could do that would cause any great rift between us', unaware that it made falling in love with Raphael sound tantamount to a crime. She only wanted my happiness and the fulfilment of my writing; she could see it was a meeting 'of the minds and of hearts'. Giving up smoking (after nearly forty years) had made her brittle and snappy, she reckoned, pausing for an admission I thought worth a thousand careful words: 'I want to say so much to you but it won't come out the way I want to say it.' 'Your father,' she told me, 'went and bought the *Guardian* – just to see.'

By contrast, when I met Raphael's family a fortnight later in North London it went swimmingly. I was in a daze of delight at a very large gathering of relatives, friends and colleagues, a party for his uncle Chimen's seventieth. With their Russian names – Yasha, Sasha, Kolya – reminding me of Tolstoy or Pasternak, and their political pasts – all the older generation, his uncles and aunts on his mother's side, had joined the Communist Party in the 1920s or 1930s to fight fascism – I felt I was encountering History with a capital 'H'. Raphael's mother and I took to each other immediately. A diminutive sprite of a woman with cropped hair, a cockney voice and an almost Maoist-blue trouser suit – was she really, as I now calculate, seventy-seven when I met her? She seemed not just a different generation from my own grandmother but a different species. My grandmother had been a servant and

had ten children; she was Victorian by comparison. Minna
hardly seemed 'old' at all. An artist, an atheist and internationalist, Minna was modern, forward-facing. I fell in love
with her too, or with the idea of her, and with the idea of my
new Jewish family.

★

On our wedding day, 3 July 1987.

I had not wanted – till then – to get married. Why marry? Why did Raphael want to get married? He wanted to marry *me*. Neither Raphael nor I had ever been married before and that was the point, but we knew it would be unpopular among many of our friends. Marriage was seen as retrograde, as relegating the woman to a subordinate position, and was exclusively heterosexual; one gay couple refused to come to the reception by way of protest. Given the orthodoxies of the left, Raphael maintained that it would be pleasingly 'countercultural' to marry. Naively, I thought getting married might connect me to the rituals of the past, and make me seem more 'normal' to my parents. I'm not sure who was the most deluded.

Plenty of people felt that the marriage was public property. One friend sent me the vows of Zhou Enlai and Deng Yingchao, Chinese revolutionaries, as a model, though privately confessed that she was otherwise 'mystified' by our decision; a colleague, whom I barely knew, stopped me on campus to ask me to justify getting married; someone I had known for years joked, 'You'll be known as the person who embourgeoisized Raphael Samuel' (and yet after he died I was also seen as a dumbing-down influence, introducing him to package holidays and television). My sister too felt let down by my not holding out against marriage. We received a score of congratulations nonetheless and wondered how to include everyone in the festivities.

Raphael offered to change his surname to 'Light'. He had never liked 'Samuel', which reminded him of the British chain of high-street jewellers (the reason why the East End villains he was interviewing thought he might have a fortune stashed away and that I was probably a gold-digger). But

'Raphael Light' sounded, we agreed, a little too numinous. I liked that his first name and his surname contained my initials, 'AEL'. It was another of those lovers' signs, part of our private Kabbalah. I kept my own name, a small enough gesture, although surprisingly unassimilable to some. Letters to 'Mrs Samuel', or even to that curious personage 'Mrs Raphael Samuel', continued to arrive throughout our life together. I agonized over whether to wear a ring; we got perfectly nice ones for under twenty pounds each.

On our wedding morning in Brighton, I expected Raphael to turn up at the register office in the Regency Pavilion wearing the open-necked pink shirt we had bought specially. It looked a treat with the navy linen suit from a local second-hand shop. 'An outfit I will hugely enjoy wearing,' he wrote to me not long before the ceremony, adding in mock apology that he seemed to have fallen 'into the ancient gender role of the man who relies on his woman to turn him out nicely'. In a nod to tradition, we spent the night before the wedding apart. Next morning there he was, newly kitted out, but in a white shirt and a red tie, something he never usually wore, and instead of the brand-new pale blue suede desert boots, a pair of clumpy black leather lace-ups. His friends had dressed him in clothes they considered more fitting for the ceremony (the red tie presumably a gesture towards radicalism). Raphael had given himself up to the collective will.

To his more bohemian friends we seemed to be having a traditional 'do' in Brighton: a hotel reception at the Old Ship, opposite where we lay on the beach that first time, a sit-down lunch and then a disco at a pub later. Few London friends were invited but neither were the extended families. To my parents, it was all slightly skew-whiff, like my punky gelled hair. We got married on a Friday, which was traditionally unlucky but more importantly put everyone to the inconvenience of taking a day off work. Raphael hadn't fancied our anniversary for ever coinciding with the Fourth of July. We wrote our own vows, and Raphael was so tearful he could hardly get through them. Instead of looking after our guests after the ceremony we strolled along the seafront to the hotel, chatting with the photographer, another solecism. (His serious, unsmiling photo of us on the pier captures a sense of embarkation.) I gave a speech at the reception, speaking warmly of how much I owed my parents, as if wanting to take them with me. Our mutual friend Ursula Howard made a splendid tiered wedding cake and iced it. Her decoration was a lovely surprise to us – a frieze of alternating symbols in pink, the feminist sign for woman, the hammer and sickle, and hearts – intended, at least in part, as a spoof. I kept the third layer, as was tradition, for a christening; years later I found it in a cake tin at the back of a cupboard, covered with green mould.

Our guests deluged us with presents, as if we were young marrieds. An anthropologist might have easily attributed them to their different tribes. My Portsmouth family and the East Enders sent the more conventional, very welcome bed linen and towels (Raphael was amazed to find the latter need not abrade the skin like sandpaper); my parents paid for the wedding drinks and bought us a Teasmade, and Raphael's family had a whip-round for a washing machine. My brother gave us a new kettle; my sister a chamber pot (the lavatory at Elder Street was outside). Old lefties sent gifts in keeping with their household gods: a huge meat platter ornamented with the crowds marching to protest the transportation of the Tolpuddle martyrs to Australia in 1834 (designed by the National Trade Union of Agricultural and Allied Workers); an original cartoon of 1835 making fun of royalty; three decorative plates from the miners' strike of 1984; a corkboard for memos, and, more to my taste, a set of beautifully figured champagne glasses from the Soviet Union. A few presents, like *The Book of Trades* from 1807 and a watercolour of John Ruskin, seemed intended purely for Raphael. More troubling was the recording of Verdi's *Otello*, the story of a cross-cultural marriage that ends in strangulation and suicide.

'You must be mad,' one of Raphael's old lovers said to me by way of introducing herself. This was our third or fourth wedding party. Unable to cope with, or afford, a grand bash, we had settled on the idea of 'organic' celebrations: a party at Ruskin, a party with Raphael's family, and so on. The Friday wedding in Brighton gave us a day to recover before we invited people to Elder Street on the Sunday in 'tranches' from 12.30 and then 6.30 onwards. First we held a wedding breakfast in the backyard in nineteenth-century style, with champagne and kippers 'off the back of a lorry', courtesy of an East End fence. Raphael was determined to cook for guests: 'tureens of cold watercress soup', perhaps, or chilled borscht 'prepared a day or two beforehand'. He was elbow-deep in beetroot on the Saturday, cooking until midnight, while I tidied and decorated the house. Otherwise the catering relied on friends bringing dishes, and neighbours offering their fridges, and helping us with the mountain of leftovers next morning as we went up and down the street, palming off food before we left for our flight.

Our honeymoon in Shetland was partly organized by Brian Smith, the islands' archivist, and by John Shaw, a Ruskin student and another Shetlander. We almost didn't make it. Arriving late for the flight to Aberdeen, the stopover for the islands, Raphael could not be parted from his work and refused to check in to the hold his grey army-surplus rucksack, with its unwieldy frame like a whale-boned corset, crammed full with lever-arch files, Berol black ink pens, reams of rough paper, a plastic pot of glue and a pair of scissors (these were the days when 'cutting and pasting' was a literal activity and long before high-security checks). Eventually his obstinate, gentle entreaties wore the staff down and we all set to, decanting everything into rapidly purchased carrier bags.

The choice of Shetland in the far north of Britain reflected Raphael's preference for the rugged and windswept. He inherited this aesthetic from his mother, a fresh-air fanatic who loved hiking and who, as a good Communist, disdained anything too soft, domesticated or pretty (later I got him on to the beaches of the Canary Islands and Crete, where he rediscovered a childhood love of sunbathing). On the ferry crossing to Bressay I tried for silent communion with the sea and sky, but Raphael broke in with endless questions about the islands, trying to get his bearings. He was more at home on Noss, sublimely bleak, whereas I burst into tears, overcome. We set off in search of puffins, warned by the local ranger to stick to the edges of fields lest we be scalped by the local skuas, or 'bonxies', anxious about their young. I was delighted to spot a puffin on the cliff edge high up, and crawled forward impressively on my stomach, like a professional. Hundreds of pairs greeted me, in a vast chattering, mocking congregation, as I looked down.

One evening in Lerwick, Raphael addressed a meeting of the Labour Party on 'Liberalism and Socialism', examining their commonalities and their differences. I was struck by how remote the audience was from the pieties of 'New Labour'. Next day we absconded to the Italian ice-cream bar. At the cottage we read Dickens's *Our Mutual Friend* aloud to each other, with Raphael falling easily into croaky cockney for the part of the 'Golden Dustman'. We went to bed and made love in the afternoon, and again at one or two in the morning, the darkness in 'the simmer dim' never quite arriving. I labelled my new diary 'Married Life Volume One!', though I was never free of the level-headed observer (superego, killjoy?) who poured cold water on my raptures. In a local shop I bought a red-patterned Shetland jumper. The assistant turned towards me politely, asking, 'And is your father wanting one too?'

On our return to London a hurricane hit the city. It swarmed up the canyons of high buildings and I woke up in the attic bedroom to the rush of sound in the chimney. Raphael was asleep. 'It's quite windy out there,' I said in an understated English way, but he did not stir. Downstairs I checked on the cat, looked outside into the street and flinched as doors slammed and dustbins overturned, their lids yammering away. In our backyard the solitary tree bent ominously back and forth; inside, the sash windows rattled in their frames. After the hurricane a financial storm followed – 'Black Monday' – when stock markets around the world went into meltdown. A hush hung over the City as the champagne bars, newly sprung up near Liverpool Street, were eerily empty. Raphael wondered, only half in jest, if we should go out for a drink and toast the collapse of the banking system. We decided it was premature.

Our wedding cake with its radical icing.

4 Moving

In our courtship days Raphael put in a plea for my keeping the flat on Albion Hill and for both our homes to become mutual, but I was already committed to buying with my friend Sue. She and I got a mortgage for a late Victorian terraced house where I had a bedroom and small study on the first floor and she two rooms on the ground; the bathroom, kitchen and sitting room in the basement were shared. The house was nearer to the London Road station, easier for my job at the poly in Falmer a couple of stops on. Much of the time I was pulled in the opposite direction, going up to London to see Raphael. In the months before the wedding I was in a flurry of moving, putting belongings in both places. It was years before I settled.

The romantic in me felt that Raphael and I should make a home together. Raphael's house, though, was very much his. He had lived there for twenty-five years, first renting in the 1960s and later buying it for a song. It had always been shared and had served as an open house and a kind of London annexe to History Workshop's activities: in *Miners, Quarrymen and Saltworkers* (1977), Raphael invites the reader to 'write to 19 Elder Street, Spitalfields, E1 for help or advice in organizing a local workshop'. For a time he was living with historian Anna Davin and her three children, Dom, Mick and Kathy (he stayed firm friends with their father, Luke Hodgkin). Then a series of lodgers and lovers came and went. Raphael mostly migrated between his desk and the kitchen. A bedroom on the second floor was like a working-class parlour, seldom used except for guests. His habit was to bivouac on the wooden floor of his study; 'Raphael never has sex,' one of his women friends had felt obliged to tell me, 'he works all night.' Curled up in a sleeping bag, he could sleep through two alarm clocks, relying on British Telecom to phone him awake. When I first stayed, he scurried up and down stairs, coming to bed with me at midnight, getting up at two, reappearing at four, and finally disappearing at five thirty to get an early train to Oxford.

The house was saturated with history. It was built in 1727 when the silk-weaving community of Huguenot refugees made their home in Spitalfields, and with its window seats, panelled walls and shutters, it was full of ghosts. Innumerable feet had hollowed out the treads of the wooden spiral staircase. As if the building were a palimpsest, endlessly written over, it bore the signs of its occupation through the centuries: the cast-iron range in the kitchen was a Victorian addition; the mezuzahs on the lintels belonged to the 1900s when Jewish families had lived there; a tiny washbasin tucked away in an upstairs cupboard harked back to its being a lodging house fifty years later. As I explored the house with its five rooms, one on each floor from the basement to the attic, the hearths reminded me how many different individuals, sometimes separate households, would have cooked, washed and huddled for warmth over the open fires.

Did the house shape the marriage? Perhaps it was the alchemical catalyst that changed us both, creating a new amalgam – the dialectical union of opposites. It gave Raphael room to take to domesticity, the pretext for enjoying some privacy and separation from a crowded life, while I, always at pains to protect my sovereignty, found myself displaced. I often felt that the house was on loan from history and I was yet another traveller in time, merely passing through. I loved the house and sometimes I hated it too.

★

Elder Street in the late 1970s; number 19 is on the left-hand side, third from the bottom.

We were not newly-weds with plans for redecoration and the fabric of the house also made it resistant to change, with the single room on each floor islanding the occupants. Raphael had already spent time in the 1980s shaping the house to his needs and beginning to beautify it. With Jim Howett, a quiet American and considerable Spitalfields craftsman, he had sanded and polished the spiral staircase and set to on the floors,

revealing the original nine-inch oak boards. Large construc-
tions of shelving took over, with sizeable Jim-built filing
cabinets beneath; books became the scaffolding of the house,
backed by ranks of the hefty black A3 ring binders Raphael
favoured. Books and files dominated every room; they were
hidden behind damask curtains or wedged into bookcases on
landings and up the stairs, even along the perilously narrow
flight to the attic, elbowing anyone who tried to pass. Loose
papers tumbled from manila folders.

Along with my books, I took my creature comforts up to
London: the sofa and the cat. The cumbersome Edwardian
three-seater, decked out in Sanderson chintz, had moved with
me from Bedford to London to Brighton. Now it struggled
up the corkscrew staircase, cracking its frame, losing a caster,
gouging holes in the plaster, which gaped to reveal the lumps
of horsehair with which it was packed, before taking up resi-
dence on the first floor. On day one, Morgan, the cat, vanished
for a time up the chimney, sheltering, we assumed, on the
ledge where boy chimney sweeps might have found a foot-
hold. Earlier feline residents, the ill-named Tess and Jude, had
come to sticky ends, so Raphael quickly penned a note to the
neighbours introducing Morgan, warning them that he was a
Brighton cat who needed time to 'acclimatize himself to his
new metropolitan surroundings' and asking that no one 'shoo
him away, as the houseproud and garden-conscious are liable
to do'.

When Virginia the lodger duly moved out, we put a mattress under the eaves. I wanted a fitted carpet up there, the
only one in the house, and was delighted and exasperated by
Raphael in the department store when he instantly lay down
on the rolls to see if their comfort matched up to my Brighton

flooring where we had occasionally made love. The attic was the one room I could paint, so I chose a deep cranberry pink. I concocted a matrimonial canopy of Nottingham lace to drape above the mattress, as if it were a four-poster. It was like waking up inside a throat infection under a mosquito net; the lace was soon abandoned and the walls redone in a less livid colour. We were four floors up from the bathroom. Raphael got even more exercise.

His unused bedroom on the second floor, the sunniest room in the house, became my study. I put my large work table where the bed once was. It was lucky that books mattered more to me than clothes, as there was little hanging space anywhere in the house. Otherwise my domestic 'improvements' were mere tinkering: an old 'Turkey' rug in the kitchen and a fireside basket chair from Brick Lane market, where second-hand furniture was splayed out on waste ground behind the stalls; and a heavy iron grate for the first-floor room, manhandled into a borrowed wheelbarrow and steered home through lines of traffic – though it hardly affected the fug of smoke generated by the open fire. Terry, a local builder and one of Raphael's East End interviewees, fixed a stone mantelpiece for connubial knick-knacks above the hearth and, with the sofa installed, Raphael invited his friends upstairs to marvel at 'the room', as we called it, neither 'drawing room' nor 'lounge' seeming appropriate.

Raphael's aesthetic leant toward the Victorian rather than the Georgian; he preferred shade and clutter to light and space. Jim had painted the shelves and cabinets in the house black and edged them with green baize; faded velvet curtains hid the window seats and shutters. A painted leather screen and crewel tapestries obliterated even more of the original panelling and an imported Victorian range served as an ornament in Raphael's study (though the one in the kitchen still burnt wood). The red quarry tiles for the floor were another new-old addition to the matchboarded kitchen, as was a back-breaking butler's sink. Old gas chandeliers were adapted for electric light. Outside, Raphael successfully made the little backyard even gloomier with rampant ivy, that darling of the moated grange. It was his only horticultural success since planting indoor plants out there by mistake. The ivy ran amok, surging up the back of the house, its tendrils working their way through the shutters and creeping into the rooms. It proliferated at the front of the house too, alongside ailing ferns in tin buckets, in the small wells under the basement windows, happily obscuring what little light came into the kitchen and giving a melancholy tinge to life even in summer.

Number 19 appeared so authentically Victorian to the television crew who filmed an episode of *The Adventures of Sherlock Holmes* outside in the street (Jeremy Brett was the cocaine-injecting, violin-playing detective in this series), that its façade needed no 'dressing' except for the antique lace they gave Raphael to shroud the ground-floor windows. By contrast, when a version of Henry Fielding's *Tom Jones* was televised in 1997, our house was not deemed 'period' enough, though it was a good twenty years older than Fielding's novel. The front door, a weighty original, was replaced by a smart cardboard cut-out which looked, to the production team at least, more in keeping with a Georgian townhouse. For a few days I left the house through two doors into a street covered with new mud. I was deep in grief at the time, so it intensified the sensation of living in a parallel universe.

At number 19 the bathroom was spliced out of the kitchen, a pine partition through which one heard every splash and gurgle. Visitors put on a brave face or never minded the eccentricity for a night or two. Some, like me, had grown up with similar arrangements; showers were still a novelty in English houses and the craze for multiple bathrooms was as yet unheard of. I bought a rubber appendage which hooked over the bath taps and produced a feeble flow of water. It struck Raphael as sheer wizardry. He proceeded to ignore it, washing his hair in the bath as before. Although one fraction of English bohemia leaves locks off bathrooms, I rapidly put on a bolt.

Only the limber and slim could easily relieve themselves. Jim had fashioned a bucolic retreat on the other side of the backyard, an elaborate, extended wooden shelter with the lavatory in one corner, over the spot, presumably, where the cesspit had been. It was entered via a pair of narrow shuttered doors of the kind swung open by swaggering cowboys in saloons, recoiling viciously on the visitant, who needed to edge in sideways. A splendid Edwardian varnished oak seat, a top cistern with ball-and-chain mechanism and a very satisfying flush were the reward. I did find myself wondering, as I donned a hat, mac and wellingtons to venture out in a downpour, how many other householders within a stone's throw of the City's office blocks were similarly placed. But I never minded much. The outside toilet had been a room of one's own in my childhood, a haven generally unknown to a family of five in a small terraced house. I would go there to cry or daydream. Blessed as I am with a very sensitive nose, I thought indoor toilets very unsavoury when I encountered them later in life, unpleasantly situated in bathrooms or next to bedrooms.

Gradually we consummated our book collections, mine quite meagre by comparison with Raphael's, but more catholic. Raphael's was the first working library I had encountered, built up around projects over the years: old school textbooks and primers; working men's memoirs and theatre lives; European and international histories; Labour history and Marxist theory; historians reflecting on their craft; English, Scottish, Welsh and Irish histories; the histories of art and architecture, county towns, tower blocks; the history of taste; books of old photographs; histories of religion, of London, of chapbooks and folk art (I was intrigued, I remember, by a large yellow tome entitled *The Early Comic Strip: Narrative Strips and Picture Stories in the European Broadsheet from c.1450 to 1825*). One leather-backed volume, with the alluring title *Vagabondia*, was much thumbed, an illustrated collection of beggars, exotic street performers and other 'mendicant wanderers', published in 1817. The massive volumes of a late nineteenth-century Bible with Gustave Doré's intensely dramatic engravings left my hands sooty with dye from their covers.

My English classics, American poets and women's writing leavened Raphael's left-wing library: his copies of Mayakovsky, Auden and Spender, Brecht and Hugh MacDiarmid, and a collection of popular verse (including a volume of temperance ballads which were once a smash hit among Methodists). I expanded his section on psychology and religion and myth – the latter two very close together in the Marxist as in the Freudian mind – while my psychoanalytic texts joined his history of sexology on the landing halfway up, a suitably intermediate zone. His novel collection was more eclectic, though again with a historical or political hard core – all of Gorky, for instance – alongside more popular writers, particularly those who lent themselves as illustration of historical topics. Mixed in with the row of *Punch* that lined the hallway were Harrison Ainsworth's historical romances, the 'silver fork' novels of Bulwer-Lytton, as well as Dickens and Hardy. We argued amicably over classification by author or century, the forces of the individual imagination as opposed to the shared influences and impact of the wider culture. In the end my Austen and Eliot rubbed shoulders with their contemporaries, and my mind took a more historical turn.

*

Raphael's house was not a time capsule or an attempt at restoration of 'period'. His liking for bare wood owed much, he said, to the 1970s rediscovery of Scandinavian pine (my Habitat kitchen table, now my desk, immediately looked at home). There was more than a smattering too of that left-wing asceticism which aimed at the simple life. He had an aversion for the 'gussied up' – no chenille tablecloths or antimacassars for armchairs in this version of the Victorian. Equally anathema was the cosmetic – a garden that was too 'kempt' – or pictures placed symmetrically, or identical cushions carefully coordinated. Much was in keeping with the ethos of William Morris, whose well-known adage 'Have nothing in your house that you do not know to be useful or believe to be beautiful' took aim at the mass production of shoddy goods. On an early visit to my flat, Raphael sniffed out that my velvet curtains were not really old and not really velvet. He fell unusually silent. I was a quick learner and they never made it to London.

The house appealed to my senses: the glow of the polished floorboards with their knots and bumps; the blue panelled room on the first floor; the tawny curtains, which hung in heavy, soft folds. But the ironies of living with bare boards, bare plaster, open fires and an outside toilet were not lost on me. During my childhood and teenage years, these were the marks of poverty. In his precious time off, my father worked to transform our cold, damp, vermin-ridden house inch by inch, hard-boarding over banisters and doors, taking down dust-gatherers like dado rails, blocking in the old fireplaces, all to reduce the layers of grime and save my mother hours of work. Fitted carpets gradually replaced the filthy job of beating rugs on the washing line; wallpaper too was a boon, papering over the cracks – they both remembered going to bed as children with a bar of soap and a candle handy to swat and incinerate the insects who crawled out of the crevices. After decades of lighting grates with coal, fiddling with paraffin heaters and singeing our legs on electric bar fires, central heating, when they could afford it in the late 1970s, was the ultimate luxury, providing a warm bathroom and constant hot water.

The first winter Raphael and I were together was a severe one. January 1987 saw twenty inches (50cm) of snow in southern England, with temperatures staying well below freezing all day (the cold even affected Big Ben's chime). I swathed myself in shawls like a mill girl, and wore two pairs of socks and a hat in bed like my grandmother, but the romance of defrosting the pipes with a hairdryer and carrying buckets of warm water across the yard to thaw the toilet soon wore off. Raphael promised me central heating as a wedding present and in due course the long-suffering, good-humoured Victor, who did the job, all but moved in. He was cautioned by Raphael not to tamper with the oak floorboards and devised a congeries of pipes in corners and over skirting boards until the house resembled a domestic version of the Pompidou Centre or the Lloyd's building, wearing its snaky plumbing on the outside. Even so, Raphael had to brave the disapproval of his conservationist neighbours, who warned darkly that the wood panelling would dry out. Only constantly replenished saucers of water under every radiator, as if for an army of thirsty cats, we were told, might mitigate this.

They need not have worried. There were plenty of draughts. Free of radiators, the spiral staircase acted as a bracing centrifuge. No doors fitted their frames, nor did the windows. Much of the eighteenth-century glass, where it survived, was cracked; there were open fireplaces on all floors; and no carpets for insulation except in our bedroom. With an outside lavatory the back door was always in use and the rusted metal cat flap set deep in its timbers, surely as old as the house itself, swung breezily, constitutionally unable to shut. None of this mattered to Raphael. He was as immune to cold as he was to illness. His only concession was a small electric fire in his study. He liked to warm his hands over it as if it were a brazier and he a chestnut seller.

I was bemused again by the sense of returning to the topography of childhood when I shopped at the local markets, as if I were still carrying my mother's string bags back from the Charlotte Street stalls in our home town. The nearest supermarket was a mile away, halfway down the Bethnal Green Road, more or less opposite the pie and mash shop where eels stirred in buckets outside. We had no car and extra shopping depended on the bus or a long walk. Only the cat partook regularly of convenience foods. Raphael would load up his all-purpose grey rucksack with Whiskas in 'industrial quantities', a phrase from his days of cooking for Anna's children. When Marks & Spencer opened a food hall in Moorgate, fifteen minutes away, I shopped guiltily for a few ready-made meals and smuggled them in.

The kitchen was pretty basic: a small fridge without a flap to the freezer compartment and an antiquated cooker with a broken regulo, which added an element of surprise to baking or roasting; also the handle to the tiny eye-level grill pan had gone AWOL. Clothes had to be washed by hand or piled willy-nilly, with the sheets, into black bin liners, as Raphael did, hoicking them in a taxi up the Bethnal Green Road to the launderette. The yard was too dark and cramped for a washing line, but an ill-tempered Eastern European tumble dryer squatted in a cloud of damp at the far end of a kitchen cupboard under the stairs. None of this prevented Raphael from being hospitable, cooking for eight or nine, and constantly putting people up. When Raphael's family gave us a washing machine – my first – it transformed our lives. It too was ingeniously sandwiched into another aspect of this cupboard and I proudly plumbed it in.

At first Spitalfields was little more than a vivid backdrop to our love affair. A few trips out to pubs on a Sunday lunchtime, and a bit of shopping, but otherwise I left the house early, plunged into the streams of commuters at Liverpool Street station, and went against the flow as I set off for my job at the poly. Compared to Brighton's hilltop vistas and the stretch of shore, Spitalfields was very built up. It was also, like the house, steeped in history. Raphael showed me the Huguenot merchant houses on the other side of Brick Lane, far grander than his own, with their airy weaving lofts and front doors framed by elaborate cornices and pilasters, though he

thrilled rather more to the damp-walled passageway of Puma
Court, a survival from the days of back-to-back housing. I
picked up a few scraps of information: Spital Square owed its
name to the medieval hospital once sited there, and the triangle of Tenter Ground was where cloth was once stretched
out to dry; like nearby Fashion Street, and the more famous
Petticoat Lane, its name bespoke the importance of the gar-
ment industry in the area. Mostly, though, Spitalfields was a
jumble of historical associations thrown together higgledy-
piggledy, like the network of alleys running into each other
behind the main thoroughfare of Bishopsgate.

I was not a historian. The district felt run-down to me, its
houses shabby and its buildings unglamorous. Spitalfields
market made it scruffy and smelly but kept gentrification at
bay. At dawn, women came up from Brixton to buy bruised
fruit and we often saw the down-and-outs shivering over
their makeshift fires and burning the wooden pallets from the
stalls, which we also filched for our grates. They took their
rest in 'Itchy Park', a scrubby bit of grass in front of Christ
Church, whose spire loomed over the area. Raphael was fascinated by every level and variety of work in the Victorian
city but especially by the travellers and wayfarers who were
so essential to urban life, from the seasonal workers and those
bringing their produce or their muscle to town, the hawkers
and dealers in all kinds of goods, to the showmen and street
entertainers, and all of the 'comers and goers' whose lodgings
and lean-tos and encampments had left little trace. I loved
him for loving the itinerant, the migrant, the vagrant. He was
an urban creature. A Londoner. But what, I wondered, was I?

★

In his basement kitchen Raphael had a cabinet of curiosities, a glass-fronted corner cupboard filled with dusty objects. Among them, a lump of coal from the Durham coalfields and a plastic National Coal Board mug; a yellow-and-black theatre programme for a performance in 1956 of Brecht and Weil's *Threepenny Opera*, 'Mack the Knife' sketched on the cover as a predatory City gent, with bowler and cane, about to fleece the poor; a misshapen pottery animal, half cow, half crocodile, made by one of the children; and some relics as old as the house itself, stems and bowls from eighteenth-century workmen's clay pipes and a coin, or a medallion, nestling in a little receptacle. Like the pipes, it was discovered when the floorboards were taken up, though I did not make much of it. Dated 1795, it belonged to 'the London Corresponding Society' and was inscribed 'United for a Reform of Parliament'. After I moved in, Raphael and I spent a morning together, shuffling a few items off into his study and replacing them with wine glasses to reflect the light. The coin stayed where it was.

The evidence of past lives lay not only in the house's fabric but in Raphael's penchant for those humble objects which were far less likely to survive in museums than the household goods of the more affluent sort. What seemed to me curios were often a way of thinking about the past, part of an argument or an interpretation of history, as well as a source for it. The three sturdy green glass bottles which stood on the kitchen windowsill were London survivals: R. H. White and Sons Ltd of Camberwell and Walworth, and Greene King of Acton W and Tottenham N, evidence of the great age of Victorian breweries; the P (Peninsula) and O (Oriental) silver ashtray we used for sugar conjured the luxury cruises between the wars. But what of the large glazed earthenware cider jar from Harry Lee, Wine and Spirit Merchant of Honiton (number 1378)? Did it belong to research into the history of drink or was it retained because it was as elegant and simple as a piece of Bernard Leach pottery? Did the rusty cowbell with its loud clapper echo a vanishing agricultural world? Some were serendipitous finds, like the National Dried Milk tin where Raphael kept teabags, or the sweet-shop jars that held coffee beans from which he made a brew of Balzacian strength. Others, like the Lord Kitchener paper napkin and the jubilee mugs, were more obvious reminders of history brought home.

More déjà vu as I recognized the blue-and-white cups and saucers from my 1950s childhood, embellished with willow pattern or English cathedral scenes. I was less enamoured than he was of pewter (the poor's man silver), though I knew that our dented milk jug with its raffia-bound handle was more than a mere adjunct to the history of everyday life. Even the poorest home had a decorative item or two, a sure sign that the wealthier classes did not have a monopoly on the aesthetic sense. Home-making was always creative, and it was generally women's work.

The house was also an archive of political imagery. Scurrilous satirical cartoons, coloured facsimiles of French Revolution playing cards, trade union posters, the theatre bill for George Bernard Shaw's play *Arms and the Man*, a striking graphic in shades of ochre and red of square-jawed Bolshevik peasants brandishing sickles and scythes, with a train of hopeful workers from across the world, fighting imperialism (the Cyrillic read 'October 1917'), and the black-and-white flyer for the 1967 'Dialectics of Liberation' with R. D. Laing and Stokely Carmichael, which Raphael attended: our walls offered a mini-history of radicalism. For Raphael, the coin of the London Corresponding Society was part of a living currency. Through his eyes I began to imagine that a weaver or a shoemaker, belonging to that clandestine association, and protesting for his rights against a brutally repressive government, had actually smoked his pipe in the basement, a Jacobin in our kitchen. By osmosis, and without particularly wanting to, I took in the history of English dissent.

Raphael marvelled that I could spend hours moving a chair into position, hanging a painting or placing a pot – in effect composing a room. I saw the danger in my own aestheticizing impulse. The pathos of objects used decoratively lay in their becoming only *objets d'art* while their historical meaning and particularity slipped away. I could see that the striking poster from the Russian Revolution had already acquired, behind our backs, as it were, a sad glamour under the Medusa eye of time, no longer either rousing or terrifying. After Raphael's death, at the back of a drawer I found a large silk scarf, or foulard, with Picasso's familiar design of doves, its colours leached. Raphael bought it at the 1951 Festival of Youth and Students for Peace in East Berlin, a sixteen-year-old ardent Communist out to celebrate the new German Democratic Republic. He had worn it, then discarded it. I framed it.

I could take only so much history. I took some of the graphic art down from the walls. Pedagogic, informative, lowly and democratic, nearly every print or engraving was illustrative of something else: a historical event or crisis, popular entertainments or occupations. I could be ruthless. I found the bawdy, satirical eighteenth-century cartoons incomprehensible and unfunny. Instead I hung reproductions, far less in keeping with the house but which could not be reduced, as I saw it, to statements about the past. I put up a

large Turner seascape full of light and, in pride of place over
the hearth in 'the room', a Man Ray poster displaying a fleshy
pyramid of three peaches, a rosy pink against a sky-blue
ground. Looking, just looking at colour has always fed me,
while Raphael felt undernourished in that respect. He attributed this in part to the old Judaic injunction against graven
images which had starved his childhood homes of pictures. I
chipped away at his more puritanical prejudices, buying cheap,
brightly coloured plates and orange and green 1920s crockery
at the market. I drew the line at the yellowing bone-handled
knives that did not cut – neither useful nor beautiful – a job lot
from Brick Lane, supplying new cutlery which lived, as it still
does now in my house, in the drawers of a dark mahogany
book-press table, of the kind once used by printers.

Upstairs in 'the room', Raphael's stereo, an excellent Aiwa,
a present from his mother, had become a museum piece. I
dusted it off and installed my record collection. Since Raphael
had no television, I rented one from Rediffusion on the
Bethnal Green Road. It came on a stand and could be wheeled
discreetly to one side. Covered with a dark red velvet curtain,
it lent a theatrical air to viewings. At first I'd sit alone in the
late evenings watching *Cagney & Lacey* or *L. A. Law* while
Raphael was working at his desk downstairs. Gradually, like
a nervous animal shyly approaching water, he came to join
me. He was amazed by the verisimilitude of detective series,
how they got the detail right in Inspector Wexford's suburban house, for instance, as if it were – and indeed it was – another
kind of historical document. Unable or unwilling to follow
plots, he interrupted excitedly with constant questions: 'Why
is he doing that, darling?' or 'Is that what people have in their
kitchens now in Surrey?' Part innocent, part sociologist, he

was thrilled by the experience but he was never going to be seduced by it.

The sofa was my refuge. I holed up for hours on that sofa, reading, and those times with a novel, being utterly lost to myself, answered that old need, a need so deep that I cannot think I have a 'self' unless fostered by these recesses, by playful oblivion. In the earliest barren tracts of my childhood illnesses, reading in bed was not only a relief from the tedium of my own company or from physical discomfort, it was revivifying, an elixir. There was always a room inside. Making that room and making homes, making a space in which to think and dream, were all connected, though I had only just, in my early thirties, begun to realize how much.

PART TWO

Marrying

When Raphael got home one day and found me lying in the empty bath fully clothed, unable to get out, he sat down alongside me on the tiled floor, rolled up a cigarette and started to chat, as if it were the most natural thing imaginable to find your partner beached up like a whale mid-afternoon. He asked no questions, nor did he urge me to buck up or pull myself together. He listened but offered no advice. My behaviour, at once theatrical and frightening, was not pathologized, though something was clearly wrong.

I knew about his own breakdowns, though not in detail. In the early 1960s, after the first New Left group fell apart, he took himself to Ireland where he all but starved; and a decade or so later, after Anna and the children left, he also plummeted. That was why, perhaps, when I seemed to be falling apart, he was concerned but not disapproving or scared. Too pat to say that a crash landing was always on the cards, that I anticipated it, perhaps even needed it; that I knew what the risks were before I fell. What did I expect (so the voice would go in my head), giving up my own place and moving into Raphael's house and his crowded life? 'I want some kind of lifting of the spirit, non-verbal, away from all this talk and analysis,' I had written long before we got married, 'another kind of atmosphere, lighter, frivolous.'

Raphael thought my misery was not purely the work of my inner demons or driven by discovering the limits of our life together, or even, as he charitably suggested, of his character. He deemed it an 'honourable' response to what was happening in Spitalfields and the threat to our neighbourhood. Far from capitalism crashing on 'Black Monday', it rose like a phoenix from the ashes, brashly self-confident. From being a backwater, Spitalfields was beginning to look like prime real estate as the juggernaut of corporate development rolled northwards. 'They keep on pulling buildings down,' I wrote in a panic to a friend, 'and I don't know what they will put in their place.' My own collapse was, as Marxists and Freudians would say, 'overdetermined' – it had more than sufficient cause.

If I still dream of Spitalfields, and wander around its shadowy streets in my sleep, it is not because it was the landscape of extremity, though it was at times – utmost happiness and deep despair – but more of dissolution, a kind of fugue or inner jazz, the place where anything might happen, and the worst did. Spitalfields unsettled me; it dislocated me. It was the place where I lost control of what I thought was my 'self', where I lost the plot, as we say.

*

When Raphael first came to Spitalfields in 1962, he was drawn by a district which seemed as yet untouched by the developer's hand. London's oldest industrial suburb, it had long been densely peopled and was teeming with history; a market had been in existence at its core from at least the start of the seventeenth century. He knew it from radical history as 'the weavers' parish', but also as a place hospitable to poor artisans, street sellers and labourers – Irish and

English alike – and to waves of newcomers through the centuries. There were strong family connections. His uncle Chimen still ran the family business set up by Raphael's grandfather off Brick Lane: Shapiro Valentine, a Jewish publishing house and bookshop. His mother had grown up nearby in one of the bleak blocks of 'Industrial Dwellings' off Wentworth Street, unadorned buildings with dark courtyards and steep stone staircases. (He showed me the modern maisonettes which now stood there.) As a boy of twelve or thirteen in the late 1940s he had leafleted and canvassed the tenements in elections when Spitalfields had Communist councillors and a Communist MP; the flats were, he said, 'citadels' of support.

In the early years of the twentieth century, Raphael's maternal grandparents, Yakov and Feigel Nirenstein, were among the many thousands who came to London's crowded Jewish quarter, fleeing the pogroms in what is now Belarus and Ukraine and was then part of 'the Pale of Settlement' of the Jews under the Russian Empire. Spitalfields had long been home to refugees and migrants. By the time I moved in, only a few traces of the Jewish diaspora remained: the synagogue in Sandys Row, a gloomy wine seller's, a delicatessen, a kosher restaurant on the Whitechapel Road among them. The warehouses and sweatshops, sometimes with their old signs not yet painted out, from the days of the 'rag trade' when the Jews had been cobblers, furriers and seamstresses, were now, like the surviving tenements, home to the Bangladeshi community; the synagogue on the corner of Fournier Street and Brick Lane, once a Huguenot chapel, was now a mosque. As they had for centuries, many people lived over their shops in houses one room deep, their windows piled up with leather goods, boxes of shoes and bolts of fabric, mostly for the wholesale trade.

The border zone between Whitechapel and Shoreditch, Spitalfields was also a buffer against the 'square mile' of the City, the financial centre of London which lay just to the south. But it had few of the excitements and little of the glamour of the West End. It was where Londoners worked rather than played. No classy restaurants, no elegant parks; no big plate-glass stores; no trendy coffee bars. Its rhythms were different from the rest of the capital. Nightlife revolved around the fruit-and-vegetable market. Lorries rumbled over the cobbles, traders carted produce, loading, unloading, shouting, joking, into the early hours. Market traders had their all-night cafés – caffs not cafés – and pubs that stayed open till dawn, though I was not intrepid enough to frequent them. Once the market had simmered down, the business world stirred. I heard the shriek of shutters going up in the offices opposite, high heels tapping past on the pavement outside. Weekends were equally topsy-turvy: no market on Saturday but also no businesses were open – deserted streets and dead hush. Raphael often went off to the British Library, but I felt weirdly out of sync in the Sabbath silence. Unusually for the time, we shopped on a Sunday at the stalls on Brick Lane.

The city spaces I knew best were tightly residential and architecturally uniform, street after street of Victorian terraced houses, with people going off to their place of work – the dockyard, the shops and various trades – sharing the same local habits and patterns for decades. My parents still lived, more than thirty years on, in the house where I was born. Though we were not religious, ours was also a parish with firm boundaries: the parish church; the Victorian public landmarks of hospital, park and prison; the local schools, like the dairy, football ground and pubs, all within walking distance. Much of London in its urban villages was like this, but Spitalfields was far less homogeneous. An architectural mélange, the Huguenot shopfronts and handful of Georgian streets, the Victorian tenements and utilitarian municipal flats, the rustic green of the Arts and Crafts façade of the market with its great glass and ironwork hall, and the bland modern office blocks – some neo-Georgian pastiche – were all cheek by jowl. With its enclave of a few houses, Elder Street was curiously stranded and felt foreshortened, almost a dead end, with a defunct garage overlooking it to the south and Nicholls & Clarke, a builders' merchant, at the other. If I went for a walk in one direction I confronted Bishopsgate, the clogged main artery in and out of the City; in the other I hit Commercial Street, which ran down to the Whitechapel Road, equally laden with traffic. I had never lived anywhere so densely urban.

Locally I knew not a soul. London friends lived at least half an hour and a Tube journey away. Our immediate neighbours were benign business people or lawyers; some were 'Tory drop-outs' – Raphael's phrase – escaping their professions; others had saved the eighteenth-century houses from destruction in the late 1970s. Different tribes again from those I was used to in Brighton. Nipping round to the corner shop in Commercial Street, run by vivacious sisters, Phyllis and Margaret, and leaving the door on the jar, was yet another throwback to my youth, but East Enders were not my parents' working class. The late-night Bangladeshi shops on Brick Lane were all-male establishments where I felt like a memsahib and was served with great courtesy if I popped in for a pint of milk. Sometimes I exchanged a word with the working girls who patrolled the passageway halfway down our street and who always said 'All right, love?' as I passed. But I missed having a community. A walk into the City, with its Stock Exchange and merchant banks, dominated by the Bank of England, took me into more unknown territory. And its denizens were commuters who disappeared at the end of the day.

Our own commuting between Oxford, Brighton and London made the small rituals of a married life hard to establish. I was living out of a suitcase, my belongings dotted around, teaching four days a week, often on new courses; the political atmosphere at the poly was grim as cuts to the staff menaced us and a new harder-edged managerialism began to insist that education measure up to the marketplace. Eating for comfort on trains, I quickly put on weight; my bike was in storage and I had little time to unwind. Backaches and headaches plagued me and I went for fruitless X-rays (never connecting my ills with hunching over the keyboard of a new Amstrad computer and spending hours staring at its eerie green screen). I began to feel tired all the time and on days off retreated to bed. Up in the attic, where the noise from the market was amplified, a good night's sleep was rare.

I thought that loving Raphael would give me a sense of purpose. I thought him a better person, 'the most moral person I've met', I wrote in my diary. I wanted to dedicate myself to him as I hadn't before to anyone. This did not mean giving up my work, though that was embryonic. But I wanted to be like him. Not to change him but to change myself. I wanted to make a different sort of life with Raphael, as he did with me. I respected his views, his politics, his learning, and that strengthened my own opinions. An idealizing love? Of course. But is it possible to love where you do not respect? Lust, yes – but love? Oh, how I wanted to change!

Raphael had done more with his life and seemed to live more fully than I. I could not compete but I tried. I stayed up all hours, took tots of rum as he did at breakfast occasionally (his nod to how nineteenth-century Londoners used to warm themselves); where he had a single glass of red wine with meals and never got drunk, I took several unthinkingly and went off to my desk to drowse. I swallowed innumerable cups of viscous coffee, no doubt contributing to my occasional dizziness and palpitations. I ate at odd times and tried to meet as many people as possible who called. Raphael worked in every available hour not spent with comrades or on cooking and housework. When he was not working, he slept. He slept with his head in his hands on his desk. Any joggling movement induced somnolence; he slept between Tube stops and once ended up fast asleep in a siding outside Oxford station until the railway staff woke him up; the comfort of plush seats in the theatre invariably sent him off. He could fall asleep in a tutorial and once, unforgivably, drifted off in the front row of a colleague's special lecture. In our years together I never saw him read a novel or poetry simply for pleasure, put on a piece of music (he listened only to 'talk radio' for the news) – he had no pastimes or hobbies. He seemed to have no need, as I did, for idling or gazing into the middle distance.

I began to feel isolated but also deprived of solitude and privacy. Wooden panelling offers little insulation from noise. Sitting in the bath, I could hear Raphael in his study pounding his ancient Olivetti overhead through the floorboards; the Central Line between Bethnal Green and Liverpool Street rumbled underneath me, almost through me. When the

History Workshop Collective gathered in the kitchen for several hours on a Saturday, I took my books or diary to the sofa but their voices could be heard floating up through the open chimney places. Fetching a coffee meant having to be sociable. 'Mean-spirited', 'pathetic', I castigated myself, weeping at my failure, as I saw it, to be like Raphael, whose way of living seemed to me to be the right way. I resented too the cockiness of Ruskin students, who came and went in 'Raph's house', though I, of all people, knew their self-assurance was often only skin-deep. Without a regional accent or dialect, I felt a fraud, a kind of bastardized, subaltern cockney (these were the years when I believed that everyone who spoke with a northern inflexion must be a Labour voter). Without being factory workers or miners or organized labour, how could my family be authentically 'working class'? Upstairs on my bed I lay seething.

In part I experienced something of what the daughter or son of a famous man might feel – being at once a protégé and a shadow. I felt, as never before, incompetent. Raphael's artless promotion of me, his uxorious delight in me, over time had a diminishing effect. Casual rudeness, the blank stares, were made worse by Raphael's insistence on introducing me proudly to everyone who wanted to talk to him (to *him*, not to his young wife) – oh, how I hated these parties which were not parties! No dancing, no getting drunk! – and the way people, *some* people, were introduced with first *and* last names. I suffered when one of Raphael's friends kept writing blithely to 'Raphael Samuel and Alison Little'. And I was indeed belittled by these feelings and ashamed.

Gradually I felt the substance of my being thin out, etiolate and evaporate. When the front doorbell rang I fled; I avoided the postman, who left a litter of rubber bands on the outside step from undoing the stacks of post delivered to Raphael each day. I never answered the phone, which rang several times a day till midnight (Raphael warned me about a lugubrious Jewish comrade who liked to ring from New York in the small hours to 'qvetch'). The house was stifling in summer and I was desperate for fresh air, protesting loudly that I was being 'buried alive in books and paper!' I insisted on breaks – weekends away in Norfolk, a week in Cornwall – but a filthy mood descended on me as soon as we made our way back through the City's faceless buildings, into the sweltering corridors of glass and concrete. On the corner of Threadneedle Street one company had created an indoor jungle in their atrium, full of exotic climbers, giant yuccas, palms and a fig, a hothouse for dealers and brokers. A few weeks later it was ripped out and modern art appeared instead. The sheer wantonness of capital appalled me.

Sometimes I felt I was living in a time machine or even a time warp, especially as Spitalfields became the focus for people doing up the houses according to their version of a more elevated Georgian past. But the late 1980s and the 1990s were gung-ho years for the City of London and inexorably, week by week, it spread its tentacles. The whole of the area north and east of Liverpool Street station was soon engulfed by 'Broadgate', a leviathan even among London's new mega-developments. I would wake to find that there was nowhere to buy dinner that day; Dewhurst, the local butcher's, and a row of shops had been razed overnight; the post office had disappeared; or the paving stones nearby were being ploughed up. In my diary I complained of living in what felt like a state of permanent revolution without domestic routines, regular hours or predictable meals. That inner turmoil found its objective correlative in the din and chaos beyond our doorstep, as the City turned into a building site.

Like millions of other Britons, I had only a vague notion of the City and of its doings: images of gents in bowler hats and pinstriped suits, carrying rolled-up umbrellas; Wimbledon stockbrokers and their stuffed-shirt bosses with houses in the country; and long-standing British financial firms where old-fashioned Toryism and the old school tie held sway. No longer. The deregulation of the banks and the removal of restrictive practices on trading and investments after the Big Bang of 1986 fuelled a new, Americanized system for doing global, not national, business. Gone were the old companies of brokers and 'jobbers', the traditional merchant banks and small 'houses', and a new era of worldwide 'financial service conglomerates' and international commercial banks was ushered in. These global corporations wanted new buildings, space to accommodate their multifunctions, and vast open-plan floors for the new breed of aggressive, bonus-driven employees, the screen and phone traders, who were turning London into a twenty-four-hour money market. In their wake came an opportunistic land grab, effectively privatizing much public space. On the edge of Spitalfields market, opposite Broadgate, the Dutch AMRO bank was one of the first to rear up, soon to be followed by other glass towers, swaggering shiny megaliths, along with high-rise blocks of luxury apartments, 'investment' properties for the international clientele as land values rocketed. On the ground we mere mortals were dwarfed by colossal cranes, deafened by the ricochet of pneumatic drills, and breathed in debris day after day. This febrile, high-octane capitalism cared very little about whose backyard it was wrecking or where that backyard was.

By way of physic, Raphael took me on local walks to get to know the area. The nineteenth century was his stamping ground. As he showed me the remains of old workshops along Worship Street, the bandstand and model dwellings in Arnold Circus, which had once been the notorious Nichol estate, or the industrial archaeology on the canal walk to Islington, I am sure that in his mind's eye he saw the thriving life of the past. My vision, though, was increasingly myopic, focused only on the boarded up and the derelict: 'Spitalfields,' I wrote in my diary, 'is a graveyard.' Superstitiously, I avoided walking under the viaduct arch of Wheler Street, hard by the railway goods yard at the top of Bishopsgate. Hundreds of the homeless had slept there, Raphael told me, and I thought a sour, dank smell still emanated from its rubbish-strewn depths, as if the odour of their wretchedness persisted. What was inside me was now sometimes outside me, and that was frightening.

Immured in the dark, cluttered, wooden box of the house, it got harder for me to go out at all. Choked by traffic and noise, I would scurry to Bunhill Fields, the nearest bit of grass, to sit next to William Blake's grave in a cemetery full of office workers at lunchtime. One day I boarded a number 22 bus, dragging each leg up the stairs to the top, hoping to get to Putney Common. I staggered off at Hyde Park, only to find that the grass expanse had shrunk to the size of a small blaring room. Propped against a tree trunk, I saw the park briefly concertina before my eyes, waxing and waning. I knew I was hallucinating. In desperation I rang Raphael from a phone booth next to the Albert Memorial, and his caressing voice, like Ariadne's thread, drew me back. I remember nothing of the journey home except that at Aldgate East I wanted to lie down to rest on the pavement amid the fast-food cartons from KFC and the rotting heap of black plastic bags. Whether I did or not, I cannot say.

Did I have a breakdown? I don't know. I found it hard to function but, except for a few days off, I went on teaching, travelling and not sleeping. Looking back, I recognize the recurring themes of not wanting to perform, of wanting to be off the treadmill, of not wanting to be envied or successful, and how familiar, even strangely comforting, it was to feel deprived and forsaken. Later, when I resumed therapy, I found a convincing narrative. But was it all a test? If so, Raphael came through with flying colours. Or a way of being taken seriously? I worried that even in this I was trying to emulate him as well as provoke him into leaving me. None of my self-analysis made my distress less powerful, less repetitive or less punitive.

★

Of course our love-making dwindled. I have always found it hard to sleep with anyone. To *sleep*. My breathing always seems to go at a slower pace. Lying next to another body is too stimulating for me, and I can easily feel bereft the minute a man falls asleep, his rhythmic breathing or gentle snores, however unobtrusive, like a slap in the face; quietly weeping as he sleeps on or poking him awake, I might start a row whose intensity is a kind of perverse love-making, bringing us back together.

My parents were openly affectionate at home but not in public, except when they posed for holiday snaps. Raphael, on the other hand, was extravagant in his demonstrations, never embarrassed to hold hands or link arms as we walked, anchoring me in a room of strangers with an arm around my shoulders. I was 'darling' (but so was his mother and his dearest women friends) and I picked up the habit. He revelled in the chance to try out old-fashioned endearments – 'sweetheart', 'honey' – and began buying valentines, including a disastrously smutty one, which he had failed to read properly. But oh, the tyranny of the double bed! I longed to sleep, actually sleep, with Raphael and went on trying, but in one way his habit of waking at dawn suited me. I could always be sure of a few hours of solitude. A bed of one's own need not mean a dead or a sexless marriage. If we had gone to bed together in the afternoons, I might wake up and luxuriate, but in the mornings I generally woke alone. A deprivation of sorts, but like all absences it gave me space. I needed that freedom, feeling easily invaded by Raphael's frantic timetable.

Raphael's desire never languished but I withdrew, finding intercourse or penetration difficult, even overwhelming. Anxiety would set in as our love-making moved towards this and when Raphael, courteous as ever, stopped, I would burst into tears or rage at him in disappointment. Again I found the scenes of reassurance as satisfying emotionally as any love-making; they brought us close and led to much talking. We had many theories about our selves and what sexual feeling was. I was taken with Freud's idea of sublimation – that there was only so much energy to go round.

My diaphragm did not make for spontaneity even when inserted before bed every night. By morning it had to be replenished and, with our improvised lives, four flights down to the bathroom was often a flight too far. We had talked of having children on our first night together, but there was no urgency from Raphael's side. He had already been a 'sociological' father to Anna's kids, whom he loved, and the role of biological father did not appeal very much – he had known too many patriarchs, he said. (He also worried that he might absent-mindedly leave a small baby on the train.) Perhaps we might adopt? He was funny and serious and good at playing with children, but neither of us much fancied reproducing ourselves. Did we want to stay one-offs?

Part of me believed then that having children and writing books were opposed. I was not ready to divide myself and my time, and feared becoming pregnant by mistake, so I went back on the pill. My lack of desire could easily flip into beating myself up: I was not good enough or Raphael did not think I was good enough to be a mother. On one train journey to Cornwall I left my seat to stand in the vestibule between carriages, thinking of throwing myself out (you could in those days). It seems excessive now, looking back, and I felt melodramatic at the time. I had no model of how to be a childless wife. All my friends of my age were having children.

Perhaps I needed a final sanctum. I was loved and desired: what more could I want? Raphael was simply, to put it differently, too much for me at times. Equally, though, outside these urgent scenes between us, it was a relief to ignore my body. I felt let off the hook of desire or having to think about how I looked. I had long ago given up wearing make-up and excruciating heels. Now I could stop worrying about sex. We never lapsed into routine and the marriage remained highly charged. And over time sexual feeling returned sporadically, as it does between couples. I know I wanted nothing more and no one else. I was fully occupied. I never stopped imagining having a child, and we might have tried later but by then it was too late. There would be time to mourn that loss too. Perhaps it is the Portsmouth in me, but I was eventually consoled by that old nostrum which others find forbidding: 'You can't have everything in life.'

Nothing stopped me writing. My diary, my thesis, reviews and articles, often at first rejected, then rewritten and accepted – a lesson of sorts in resilience. I also poured out poetry full of images of disgust and self-loathing, which I showed Raphael, including an especially pungent one about rotten fish. Rather better were a few lyrics I called 'London Pavement', identifying with the tatty buddleia on railway embankments and the weeds that managed to grow between cracks in the paving. I was reading Virginia Woolf's diaries and thinking about suicide, about what brought people to that point, but I feared going back into therapy in case it dismantled me further.

I sent a poem about my needing to evolve – I was 'a fish out of water' – to a new friend, Masha Enzensberger, a Russian émigrée and translator, whom I had met through Raphael. Masha was full of warmth and laughter, unfazed by my emotional states. We walked on Hampstead Heath and talked poetry and relationships, and about how rocky life could be. She introduced me to the poems of Osip Mandelstam, whom she translated, and to the memoirs of his wife, Nadezhda, *Hope against Hope*, with its searing account of Soviet repression. Masha replied to my poem by sending me one by her mother, the poet Margarita Aliger, who still lived in Moscow. In 'Two', the speaker can't take her eyes off a couple quarrelling on a tram. They are 'shamelessly indifferent to strangers' and she envies them:

> They don't even know their good fortune,
> and not knowing is a part of their luck.
> Think of it. They are together. Alive.
> And have the time to sort things out and make up.

I had the grace to realize it was a gentle corrective. She had said little about her past and in 1991, when she took her own life, and *History Workshop Journal* published an obituary, I discovered that her father, whom she had barely known, was the author Alexander Fadeyev, one of the founders of the Union of Soviet Writers. Fadeyev was a cultural commissar, one of Stalin's elite, responsible for imposing the correct political line on writers and artists, an ideologue who did little to protect those whose work he admired when they were faced with persecution, exile and liquidation, Mandelstam among them. Fadeyev killed himself in 1956. Aliger's poem was written that same year.

*

In Spitalfields I began to feel those feelings which I had felt periodically all my life and to call them by their names: sadness but also despair, a sense of the meaninglessness of things, of transience and of my own uselessness. It was the place where I could no longer not feel them. A repertoire of feelings, quite ordinary in themselves but that were for me, as for many others, unacceptable. If I say I felt safe to feel them, that denies the element of risk. It was – and is – risky letting such feelings surface. Sometimes I had no choice and was overwhelmed; I felt leaky and cried a lot. I could not contain myself. Then the mild depression would become full-blown paralysis. I couldn't dress myself or put on shoes; I was weighed down by weariness in every limb. I could not speak. I imagined hurting myself. I wanted to die but was too tired to kill myself.

Looking back, before I consulted my diaries, I imagined this beginning a couple of years into the marriage. I fancied it came neatly halfway, a cusp on which the marriage turned. In fact depression, or the variety of woeful, hateful moods, the uncontrollable weeping, and inertia associated with it, seeped in almost immediately, soon after we came home from honeymoon. Actually it was happening during the courtship, because 'it' – those feelings – had always been there, had always been waiting, those demons in the shadows, those annihilating voices that tell you of your worthlessness. Being loved seemed to call them forth. I knew I wasn't worthy of that love.

None of this is unusual. It is so common, so human, I should say, as to appear banal. Anyone who has fallen in love knows that their lover loves their best self, and over time that idealization, glorious and even necessary, will start to fade and tarnish. I was not depressed because Raphael was at last seeing how truly horrible I was, his 'radiant' Alison besmirched by sulks and temper, though this distressed me. I was depressed because I could not bear to see myself. I was beside myself. Raphael had learnt to live with his demons. His phobias and neuroses plagued him and caused unhappiness but at fifty they were familiars. I, though, was in a state of shock. All the time I lived alone I had apparently coped well. I was lonely sometimes, but my life had been bounded and controlled: my flat, my work, my friends and relationships.

Some of my losses were generic, the losses of modern
people in the late twentieth century: displacement from the
culture of home; loss of family and loss of place – that inter-
mittent sense of exile which seemed too grandiose a word for
my own migrations. I was becoming the sort of woman I did
not recognize. That was an excitement but also disorientat-
ing. I could not make sense of living in Spitalfields, and, yes,
it was like being sucked into a vortex but that force was inside
me too. I was a child again, infantilized by jealousy, rage and
helplessness. I blamed Raphael for abandoning me. I blamed
myself for blaming him. And I found myself and my feelings
(such a measly 'me-me-me' kind of word) both riveting and
tiresome.

I tried cultivating our own backyard, planting window
boxes with tulips and lobelia from the Columbia Road flower
market. I had Anna's tree, which overshadowed it, cut down
(not too symbolic an act, I hoped); its roots had exhausted the
soil of the single flower bed. In went columbine and lilies and
sturdy shrubs, a spotty dicentra and a spiky, fragrant maho-
nia, ugly but indestructible. I dreamt of an empty white room
with the sea beyond, but I settled for sitting on one of the iron
chairs in the little patch of sunlight in the backyard, doing
nothing but feeling the warmth on my face. One day I
watched a spider make its web and felt immensely cheered.
The traffic hummed in the distance, an aeroplane took wing
overhead, a car door slammed far off and water rushed down
next door's drainpipes – '*rus in urbe*', Raphael said, was what I
needed, the illusion of the country in the city. My garden in
Brighton floated before me, a mirage of an oasis. Or of 'the
bright field', as the poet R. S. Thomas calls it, the place where
one turns aside.

Over time I learnt to see my depression not as an 'episode' but more as a feeding of those feelings into my life, like black milk, so that I would always recognize them as part of who I had been, was and would be. Part of my normality. I knew I was lucky. I was cared for; I had loving friends and a loving husband. I had money and a roof over my head. And when I had the space to write and think I no longer felt, as my diary put it, that the city was 'a dark throat into which I was being poured'. Eventually the worst passed. I joined the human race.

What *is* a breakdown? 'Catastrophic disillusionment', the psychoanalyst Adam Phillips calls it, the collapse of one's own ideals, of the ego as it has been 'cobbled' together, or, to put it differently, a disenchantment or awakening, the dispelling of one's romance with one's self. Perhaps this could only have happened to me in Spitalfields; only in that besieged environment, in that house, in that marriage, with that man – but should I curse or bless? Without Raphael would I eventually have plunged deeper and for longer? Or stayed brittle and competent, and perhaps more afraid? There was another cold comfort. When Raphael died I began to see the difference between depression and mourning, and, scraped from the bottom of the barrel, that knowledge is worth having, if only in small measure, and bitter though it is.

6   Foreigners

Since our initial breakfast of tomatoes stewed with garlic, piled on to bread studded with caraway seeds and washed down with a nip of vodka, I felt like Alice in the looking-glass world of 'eat me, drink me', happy to try all the potions and concoctions on offer. I learnt to enjoy the mixing of sweet and sour in Raphael's dishes, his 'tzimmes' – carrots cooked in honey and lemon juice – or his borscht with smetana, sour cream. In Blooms on the Whitechapel Road I ate my way through a plate of watery cabbage stuffed with mincemeat – just to see – and at Marks, the local delicatessen, Raphael introduced me to matzo crackers and 'kicckles' (kekkeleh), sweet biscuits dotted with raisins to be spread with cream cheese, though I found the other little 'noshes' of rollmops and gherkins less to my taste. We bought rye bread locally, or challah, an eggy loaf baked only for the Jewish Sabbath, and made forays to the Beigel Bake on Brick Lane, open all night for the cab drivers and market traders. Long before bagels became a supermarket staple, we would take home a paper bag of a dozen, so moist and warm from the oven that the dough had to be prised apart.

Raphael's Jewishness was for me part of his romantic appeal. I was delighted when his syntax took on a Yiddish inflection: 'Will you come with?' he'd say, or he'd offer to make me a 'goggle-moggle' when I was ill, a mix of milk, honey and eggs, inherited from his mother's mother, who had lodged with them when he was a boy. I was intrigued by Elkan, the Hebrew first name on his birth certificate, and by his habit of tutting, 'tsui, tsui, tsui', as a sign of approval, hoping to ward off evil, the opposite of my usage. With his shrugs and gesticulations, his extravagant 'no, no, no, no' and his almost melodramatic language – Raphael was never down or a bit miserable but 'utterly done in', never had too many commitments but was 'absolutely in a pit', never loved people but 'adored' them – I found him wonderfully foreign.

If marrying took me further away from my particular English upbringing, it seemed to make it easier for Raphael to visit his extended Jewish family. There had been bitter arguments and estrangements and throughout the 1960s and 1970s Raphael had found congenial homes in other collectivities and alternative households. Like him I distrusted the biological family, with its tendency toward the authoritarian and the possessive. For us the family remained a 'Dear Octopus' (the title of an interwar English comedy by Dodie Smith), its tentacles affectionately gripping its members. Had I noticed, Raphael remarked to me one day with some amusement, that at the end of a meeting with his relatives someone would invariably ask, 'But when are we going to *see* you?'

Raphael maintained that he had felt foreign only since marrying an English woman. To be foreign is to be in a relationship; one cannot be a foreigner alone. Our differences, though, were not equivalent; forged in the crucible of the family, they were also shaped, or warped, by the impress of the wider culture and its patterns of power. Romance skates heedlessly over history, its fissures and abysses; it liberates us, temporarily at least, from the rigid stories of ourselves and where we came from, the Montagues and Capulets, and the murderous legacies of hatred, fear and disgust. To put it differently, and less dramatically, Raphael and I fell in love, as you do, with fantasies of the other's otherness.

★

I so much associated Jewishness with food that I was taken aback when Raphael announced, before we first visited his mother, that she could not cook. After the breakdown of her marriage to Raphael's more Orthodox father, she had abandoned cookery, heavily bound up in religious ritual, as she had bourgeois comfort. An air of faded modernism hung over Minna and Bill's house, a 1930s semi on a road out of Princes Risborough, a small town in Buckinghamshire. The fitted kitchen, once smart and up to date, had seen better days, the pale wood arms of the Ercol chairs were sticky and the parquet flooring scuffed. Minna retained enough Jewish housewifery to roast a chicken (I had lapsed from my vegetarianism), and she gave us the liver as a pâté on Carr's Table Water biscuits. She and Bill generally ate plain fare, a stodgy English diet, with bacon a particular treat. Though she had grown up in the East End speaking Yiddish with her parents, I don't recall her ever playing with Yiddish in her speech.

In the late 1930s, when she became a Communist, Minna renounced Judaism, a religion she no longer believed in and thought reactionary. 'Being against God' was one of the commandments she handed on to her son, who at eight years old became, he wrote, 'a true believer' – in Communism. Judaism and progressive politics were at odds in their eyes: the one backward-looking, clannish and patriarchal; the other future-orientated, universalist and egalitarian. Barnett,

Raphael's father, made it a condition of Minna's having custody that Raphael would go through his bar mitzvah. Apparently the thirteen-year-old cheerfully recited from the Torah with a copy of Tom Paine's *Rights of Man* tucked under it. Minna chose not to go to the synagogue. Inevitably Raphael's father remained a shadowy figure to me. An affable, clubbable man, who became more pious, or frum, as he grew older, he died in 1971. His family, Raphael believed, had come from Odessa before settling in Wales, in Tredegar. Holidays spent in Wales were among Raphael's happiest childhood memories. He longed to be Welsh and spent hours as a child practising the lilt in the speech.

If the family is the cradle of identity, then Raphael's was rocked by several hands. While Minna worked in a factory during the war, Raphael was sent off to progressive, slightly wacky boarding schools, wholly immersed in communal activities with other children. He was a lonely child, deeply homesick, seeing his mother only at weekends. Back in London in the holidays, his first proper home was with Minna's sister Miriam and her husband Chimen, Raphael's mentor and 'the patriarch of our family Communism', as he put it in *The Lost World of British Communism*. As the oldest male cousin, Raphael was hugely 'fussed' (a positive word for Raphael), his precocity in argument – including Marxist dialectics – and in book learning encouraged. Twelve close members of the family were in the Party, as were nearly all their friends. Alec and Ray Waterman, both from Poland, gave him another home; their sons, Peter and David, became firm friends and Ray was another 'mother' I needed to meet. Communism was their 'gathered church', paradoxically creating a huge circle within a select band of believers, and making his childhood in some ways less divided than in many more conventional families whose marriages were intact.

Our visits to Chimen and Miriam's house near Parliament Hill in North London were always animated group occasions: the older generation – Minna's sisters and their husbands – but also several cousins, second cousins, grandchildren and family friends. The table was always laid and food could not be refused. Miriam and Chimen had kept kosher all through their Communist years (and kept the extent of their radical politics from many of their more religious friends). I noted the two sinks for washing dairy and meat dishes separately and the cutlery in different drawers; each week a Sabbath meal was held and a Seder at Passover. Chimen came from a line of distinguished rabbis and a touching photograph of four generations of Abramsky men – Chimen with father, son and grandchild – stood out in the family gallery. Neither Raphael nor Minna observed any ritual; Raphael would never have worn a yarmulke or attended a Seder (and of course he 'adored' bacon). Although tempers no longer flared, conversation sometimes veered on to thin ice. Like the rest of the family, Miriam and Chimen had long left Communism behind, but they had become increasingly critical of left-wing politics. A scholar of Marxism, radical history and philosophy, Chimen was now Professor of Hebrew and Jewish Studies at University College London, and a Zionist. Deeply involved in anti-colonial campaigns, Raphael had deemed the Six Day War a war of occupation; discussion of Israel was taboo. We steered clear of explosive topics and took lemon tea in glasses with a slice of strudel.

As a newcomer and an outsider, I found the Communist past as remote and fascinating as Chimen's wonderfully guttural Russian accent, as foreign as the gefilte fish or as the kissing on both cheeks. The family's warmth and openness reminded me of the regular confabs in childhood at my grandmother's, where a dozen of us cousins might congregate with all our parents in tow. But mine was not a child-centred family. We children were warned against 'showing off', expected to be seen but not heard, and formed our own confederacies, often in league against the grown-ups. My parents' marriage was the permanency and we, the children, learnt early to be independent. It was a weaning that I felt, at different times in life, as both a liberation and a loss. When I first encountered friends tightly swaddled by parental attention and expectations, subject to endless emotional blackmail, I was appalled. It took many years for me to think there might be a middle ground. In Raphael's family, every child's achievement was flaunted and praised. At the time we relished a TV advertisement for British Telecom (BT) featuring a doting Jewish auntie – 'Beattie' – played by Maureen Lipman. On the phone she consoles a crestfallen nephew who has failed all his exams – except pottery. 'Pottery!' she crows. 'Everyone wants plates!' And sociology: 'You got an 'ology! You got an 'ology – you're a scientist!' Now I could be one of those children!

Chimen's learning was immense; a book collector and erstwhile bookseller, he had filled his home with even more dusty tomes, precious volumes, pamphlets and manuscripts than Raphael had at Elder Street. A steady stream of scholars visited from across the world. This was a family which prized intellectual achievement. If I had even the skimpiest review in the papers or made even the briefest contribution to a radio programme, first Minna, then Raphael's aunt Sarah would ring, or Chimen would write to congratulate me. Sarah and her husband, Steve, were editors of a Faber series of children's stories collected from across the globe; Ray Waterman, Minna's close friend, had published two novels in her sixties (under the name Ruth Adler). I sent her some of my poems and we met for elegant lunches at her Willesden flat, weighing up the difficulties of being a writer if you were a woman. I told her that Raphael and I shared the housework but she was dubious: 'Who decides when the curtains need washing?' she wrote to me. I did not tell her that we never bothered.

My relation with Minna, on the other hand, hardly felt familial. I never thought of her as other than an equal, though I remember how startled I was early on when she took me to one side, grasped both of my wrists, looked into my eyes and asked if my intentions were honourable. Like Raphael, Minna loathed deference of any kind and the trappings of respectability. Along with housekeeping, she had abandoned much that was expected of women of her generation. She never wore heels or frocks; her slacks and trouser suits were variations on a theme, though sometimes enlivened by a frothy white blouse, a brooch or earrings. She wore no make-up except an occasional slash of lipstick. She was always frank but never one for small talk; she disliked 'navel-gazing' (another legacy from the Party, I imagined). Her gift was for friendship rather than intimacy. Bill was the humorist, lightening Minna's intensity. Bill wrote poetry and was an extensive reader while Minna hardly read at all, except the newspaper, as far as I could see. Pride of place in the sitting room was given to a shabby grand piano, although she wrote her music on an upright in the garage, to save Bill and her neighbours from the cacophony.

Minna's second marriage, to a Liverpool seaman turned engineer, and their living away from the capital, put her at a tangent to the family but she had long ploughed a separate furrow. Her experience during and after the war, employed in a factory and active in trade unions with her fellow workers, was at a remove from the Party intellectuals in London. Her love life was singular too. She had been that rare creature, a Jewish divorcee and a single mother; after several unhappy love affairs she fell for Bill, a married man, and it was years before they could wed. The marriage was tumultuous at times. Bill was a heavy drinker and belligerent with it, apt to needle people into rows when he was in his cups. Trips to London on their part generated frantic anxiety and endless preparatory calls between Raphael and his mother, trying to dovetail lunch in one of Bill's old boozers with Raphael's schedule of teaching, travelling and appointments. In the pub Minna fretted out loud as to whether Bill was happy, which exasperated Raphael and filled him with pity. Bill too was rattled by the placating and infantilizing; he both wanted and did not want to be the centre of attention. I felt some sympathy with Bill. Minna's music had taken over their lives as politics had her first marriage.

One morning in the garage Minna showed me the symphony she was writing, enormous quantities of notes on the stave. It was beyond my sight-reading skills but her dedication filled me with hope – not only that she went on working in her seventies but was utterly serious as an artist. The première of the symphony at the Proms in the Royal Albert Hall in her eightieth year was a fairy-tale occasion. We sat stock-still, at first electrified then exhilarated by its volcanic energy, her music a far cry from what Bill, a veteran of

many experimental concerts, dismissed as 'the plinkety-
plonk stuff'. Sensuous and aggressive, lyrical and percussive
by turns, it was high voltage, the stormy surges of orchestral
colour followed by serene, soaring passages and haunting
snatches of melody. When all the in-laws came together at a
celebration for her birthday, hosted in London by the Society
for the Promotion of New Music, the Jewish relatives, of
course, arrived with plates piled with food. Raphael was up at
dawn, skinning a mountain of tomatoes for imam bayildi, a
Turkish dish. We carefully carried the huge foil-wrapped
platter high above our heads, hoisted aloft like a princely
child, and wove our way apologetically through the custom-
ers on the ground floor of Debenhams department store on
Oxford Street, the quickest way to reach Stratford Place.

★

Minna was born in 1909, Raphael and my parents between
the wars and I a generation later. Raphael's fancy was of me as
'the Portsmouth girl' (my age and Cambridge University
notwithstanding) and as 'the pleasure principle', this last
owing much to the voluptuous sofas which Raphael had
noted gracing all my family's homes: 'I look forward to a
lifetime of lolling,' he quipped in his wedding speech. I
was, in his imagination at least, a proletarian and yet a free
spirit. But my role was more often that of a go-between or a
bridge between different worlds and the gulfs were frequently
too wide.

My parents shared memories with Raphael of the Second
World War, of the bombing, being evacuated and of ration-
ing, but dip into their lives at any point and they were poles

apart. Raphael spent many holidays in adolescence with his cousin Batia in Paris, a supporter, though a critical one, of the French Communist Party; her husband, Sasha, had been killed by the Nazis, after surrendering in 1940 in obedience to the Party line at the time. Raphael's family and their connections were cosmopolitan, with a number of languages between them — Russian, Polish, German, French and Yiddish. No one in my immediate family went 'abroad' before the mid 1970s (my father's time in Cairo during the war was of a different order of being). Leaving school at thirteen and fourteen, those of my parents' ilk were not taught foreign languages. I too did not think of myself as European. Europe was 'over there' — 'the Continent'.

While Raphael was a student at Oxford, campaigning for the Communist Party in the early 1950s, my father worked all hours in the worst kind of labouring jobs, including on the roads; my parents had two children by the time my mother was twenty. Raphael said that back in the 1940s and 1950s, he and his fellow cadres would have dubbed her sprawling family — she was one of ten siblings — among the 'unrecruitables': as unlikely to attend a political meeting as to go to church, and most likely to be found in the pub. But families are never homogeneous and my mother ran a tight ship in her own home, keeping us all afloat. She budgeted on next to nothing for school uniforms (borrowing from the 'Provy', or 'Provident' insurance cheques paid off weekly), got us regularly to the public libraries and, while we owned few books, she was devoted to reading. My parents wanted, like many who grew up in considerable poverty, to give their children more than they had, but social mobility was not so much the aim or aspiration as secure employment and a roof over our

heads. Of the twenty-odd cousins in Portsmouth, I was the
only one to go to university, though my sister Sandra had
blazed a trail, the first ever to leave home, off to teacher-
training college in 1968. These were new worlds for all of us.

'Class' was not a word I remember my parents using much
in my childhood, though a sense of injustice was strong; ours
was the natural antagonism of 'us' and 'them'. 'They' were
'the other half': the naval officers and building contractors,
'the bosses' and a sprinkling of professional people in a city
dominated by the dockyard and its adjacent trades. 'They'
were 'posh' or 'stuck-up' and we rarely met 'them' in our
urban village in Portsmouth; they lived across the invisible
equator, in genteel Southsea. Fratton, our district, was
Labour, but being Labour was social rather than ideological.
We went to the Labour Club for a drink on Sunday dinner
times or an occasional show (I longed to play Eliza in *My Fair
Lady*); 'selection boxes' crammed with chocolate were issued
to us children at their Christmas party. My mother shopped
at the Co-op for the cash 'divvy', or dividend, and for a spell
I sang in the Co-op junior choir. 'If only the Labour Party
could be like you, darling,' Raphael once said to me. I was
unsure what he meant, except that it was a compliment. I
thought the Labour Party left-wing but soon realized that for
Raphael it was 'revisionist', reformist, the Party that had long
ago given up on socialism.

In Portsmouth, left-wing politics meant militant trade
unionists: Mick McGahey or Jimmy Reid, both Scots and
Communists, were household names and constantly on the
television. My father was briefly a shop steward and a mem-
ber of the GMBTU (General Municipal Boilermakers Trade
Union), but my father's older brother, my uncle Bob, a skilled

welder, was the 'politico'. He lived outside the city and had a
car (a rarity then), and was to me a glamorous figure, with his
Van Heusen shirts and handmade Church's shoes, his RAF
past and his mathematical mind. He always arrived with a box
of Black Magic chocolates for my mother, and then they would
lock horns in ferocious arguments over whether men should
strike: the word 'capitalism' was often on his lips, and 'three
children' often on hers (he had none). When he was in his
seventies, Bob was made an example of by a vindictive magis-
trate for refusing to pay the new poll tax. The few months he
spent in Lewes prison all but broke him. Not surprisingly,
when Raphael met him, they got on like a house on fire.

The idea of a political culture which infused every aspect
of life, including one's pleasures, was totally alien to us.
Despite Raphael's childhood love of Charlie Chaplin, Buster
Keaton and Laurel and Hardy, many of his cultural tastes
were coloured by a lingering sense of the United States as the
anti-Christ, capitalism incarnate – not so much an anti-
Americanism as a resistance to Atlanticism, the unwanted
dominance of the US over British politics and the economy.
In the 1950s, when, with his friend Stuart Hall, Raphael
launched a Soho coffee bar, 'The Partisan', with a roster of
left-wing speakers and debates, it was meant as an antidote to
what they saw as the mindlessness of London's newly popular
American milk bars. My parents shared some of this prejudice
against so-called American commercialism or brashness, but
they looked to the US for their entertainment. They danced
to the big bands, listened to Nat King Cole and Frank Sinatra,
Peggy Lee and Lena Horne. Hollywood film offered them
uncondescending images of ordinary guys or tough women –
Bogart and Bacall, Jimmy Stewart, Bette Davis and Barbara

Stanwyck – a more democratic, demotic alternative to a British film industry where people like themselves would be cast as adenoidal servants or in 'character' parts.

Minna was even more of a purist than Raphael, especially about music, though Bill infiltrated some trad jazz ('Minnie the Moocher' and 'Franky and Johnny') into their record collection alongside the albums of Soviet songs which had not been played for years. I hit the right note one evening at their house with my rendering of English sea shanties – 'We'll rant and we'll roar like true British sailors' – at full throttle. My folk tradition, though, was an invented one. Radio programmes at school had taught me these English ballads (inspired, it turned out, by Ewan MacColl, collector and performer, and a close comrade of Raphael's). None of it was what we sang in the pub in Portsmouth when I was growing up: a medley ranging from the Boer War to the Beatles. I was silent while Raphael, Minna and Bill conjured stirring lyrics from the *Little Red Songbook*, the compilation of tunes used by the Industrial Workers of the World, a radical US labour union, also known, confusingly to me, as the Wobblies. My protest songs began with early Dylan and Joan Baez (I once warbled a solo of Donovan's 'Universal Soldier', an anti-war anthem, in school assembly), but my musical tastes were mongrel. In my college folk club I included Pentangle and Fairport Convention in my repertoire and then went off to the college disco to bop to Alice Cooper and Bowie. Like his mother, Raphael knew next to nothing about 'pop'.

As a child and young man, Raphael remained very close to his mother and family – ideologically and culturally. I, on the other hand, grew up in a far more liberal British culture than my parents. I watched student unrest and the marches for the civil rights movement on the TV, wrote poems against Vietnam and the Bomb, and proposed in our debating society at school that 'Yes, I would marry a black man' (though I knew not a single one). At sixteen I annotated my copies of *The Female Eunuch* and *Sexual Politics* heavily; I read E. F. Schumacher's *Small is Beautiful* and worried about the planet and 'pollution', a new nightmare. Morally abstract my views may have been but they were not wholly naive. The cold war was a fact of political life as well as the stuff of spy films and novels. I learnt about the Soviet labour camps from reading Solzhenitsyn's *One Day in the Life of Ivan Denisovich* and, later, *The Gulag Archipelago*. I read *The Communist Manifesto* and wrote to the Chinese embassy for copies of *China Today*, but knew from my sixth-form study, comparing the French and Russian revolutions, how rapidly revolution could descend into terror. In 1972, when I was seventeen, the young and fiery Bernadette Devlin, MP for Mid Ulster and an Irish civil rights leader, was a heroine. Ron Powell, not quite a boyfriend, took me to the Irish club in Portsmouth. I learnt rebel songs, including the controversial 'The Patriot Game' by Dominic Behan with its tirade against 'John Bull's tyranny' and its indifference to shooting at police. My parents preferred the less incendiary version by the Clancy Brothers or the Dubliners' 'McAlpine's Fusiliers', a tribute to the Irish navvies, men like those my father worked with.

I was often confused by my mother's attitudes (my father was more liberal and a far less vehement character, though he never contradicted her in my hearing). She was fascinated by Jewish history, for instance, as she was by Irish music; she had Sophie Tucker records and loved 'My Yiddishe Momme'; she kept a copy of *Exodus* by Leon Uris but, as with the saga novels of Maisie Mosco or the musical *Fiddler on the Roof*, I suspect that she was most moved by the celebration of family and of survival, and a nostalgia for a lost world. She was drawn to the plight of the Confederates and of Scarlett O'Hara in *Gone with the Wind* but admired Paul Robeson and Dr Martin Luther King (in her eighties, she was keen to see *Twelve Years a Slave*). She was on the side of the underdog, supported women's rights and was unfazed by homosexuality; she loathed monarchy and the church, so was hardly a Tory, but was capable of expressing every racist stereotype, her fellow feeling for the oppressed swiftly curdling into bile. For all her sympathy, did she also envy the attention paid to the deprivation of others? She had had a very hard childhood, the ninth child, the fourth of five daughters. Did she sometimes feel robbed of her own suffering, upstaged, as it were? Ultimately, when threatened, she fell back on the tribal and the atavistic, insisting that 'you should stick to your own kind'.

Yet none of her children did. My sister married Ian, a teacher of French and Spanish, a man who had been a priest, first an Anglican and then a Catholic and was to be reordained (he was also miles older than her); my brother's wife, Anita, was half German. Anita's mother, Ricky, was a war bride and liked me to speak German with her at family dinners. Raphael was in good company.

And me? The sheer fortuitousness of learning German, not French, at school, made Germany the first place I travelled to abroad, in the mid 1970s, my first romance with a culture of deep seriousness, where I could discuss philosophy, politics and poetry with other young people and without English embarrassment. From a young age I knew that its history was traumatic and utterly riven. Raphael and I never talked about the Holocaust. The books on the subject, from Anne Frank's diary to Primo Levi, histories by Martin Gilbert and Lucy Dawidowicz, were all mine; I had watched both the first airing of *Heimat* and of Claude Lanzmann's epic, *Shoah*. In late 1980s, when I first saw the photographs of Roman Vishniac, those Jewish children caught in the shtetls of Eastern Europe fifty years earlier, was it mawkish on my part to see Raphael in those faces and to realize that in any other part of Europe he too would likely have perished? I did not discuss it with him.

Raphael's learning and scholarship seemed to me to be bound up with his Jewishness and his family's culture. Did I also identify it with victimhood and had that also attracted me? Such thoughts tormented me. One night in Elder Street I dreamt that I was a Nazi, and woke up in a sweat; another that I was at the bottom of a pit with bodies being shovelled on top of me. The desire to be a victim, to account for my own woundedness – this is hardly original, and certainly more palatable than the desire to be the perpetrator. My garish dreams were a kind of psychic kitsch, the unconscious knowingly in poor taste, restaging themes from childhood too – about being bullied and not fighting back – borrowing the scenario of atrocity and total abjection for my own psychic ends. Raphael was intrigued by the dreams but not that much.

★

Of course I romanticized the Jewish family, exoticized them, idealized them. And they were not a 'they'. Yet families do create a common culture and, welcoming as they were, I thought my own migrations would be understood by them, that they would realize I had left the hearth I knew as a child. Cosmopolitan, they were also strangely parochial, turned inward, or so it seemed. I suspect that my home culture was largely foreign to them – the drinking to get drunk, the dancing and the verbal banter or jokes about sex. They kept no pets and showed little interest in sport. As a boy, Raphael had been a football fanatic (following both Arsenal and Spurs) but he could not remember anyone in the family filling in the Pools coupons or going to matches. I tried teasing an uncle in his eighties once, as I did all my male relatives, treading that thin line between affection and aggression. He instantly took offence, mimicked my flat vowels and derided my work. I stood up for myself but it was so extreme a reaction that Raphael and I both wondered if his mind was going. Raphael wrote to him the next day, extremely distressed. In the post came a pair of trousers with a note, a bizarre peace offering: perhaps, if only in his unconscious, he thought Raphael's wife wore them too often.

Only Minna, passionately in love with her proletarian Bill, could see me in a clear light but her own marriage was too hectic for more than occasional glimpses. I frequently felt ghostly at family gatherings. I was full of talk and laughter but I remained an unknown, spectral in my self. It was a good position from which to take so much in. It repeated, as I came to realize, my place in my own family, watching and listening, sitting on the fence.

And then there was always my own particular affliction as time went on: that sense of being witness to a disappearing world, that world of the elders, those who knew the world before 1939, who were young people then, full of idealism, seizing a new politics. I see them before me now, all long gone – Chimen, Minna, her sisters Miriam and Sarah – not all easy with me, this unknown, but tolerant because Raphael loved me and I seemed to be making him a good wife, making a home for their wild wunderkind, their special soul. Chimen, who still ruled the roost with his judgements, absolute and dismissive, innocently and relentlessly name-dropping and reiterating stories of his considerable achievements (and who cooked me little lunches when we were both bereaved); Miriam, who was closer to a protective mother-in-law than Minna, so much less family-orientated, ever was; and Sarah, hair dyed, scarf draped, bedangled with earrings like a fortune teller, smiling and direct.

I was of the family and yet never quite in the family. One Christmas after Raphael's death, after maybe a dozen years of knowing them, I sat eating pudding, comforted, chatting, and suddenly Sarah, out of the blue, announced in her gravelly London voice, 'Well, Alison, you are almost one of the family now,' as if up to then it had been only a masquerade, fooling no one. Voices, of course, immediately raised in protest. But she was right. I was only 'almost'. Not by history or culture. Only by marriage, that fragile, tentative bridge, a sideways link between foreign lands. Bridges that can be burnt as well as built. What did I know of their past? I had reach but no depth.

Truths, half-truths: a memoir is only ever a fragment of the story. After Raphael died I relied on my in-laws as I did on my friends, leant on them and their many kindnesses. Perhaps what is more remarkable than the chasms between us all is the finding of common ground. Ultimately there was no rift between Raphael and my parents. They learnt to understand each other better. He let my mother mock him and fuss over him as best she could. She gave him gloves and scarves, which he generally left on trains, and they even exchanged cookbooks. She shared his love of history and she learnt, as my father did, to love him for his love of me and for his gentle steely self. Raphael stayed up with my father into the small hours talking and I tried not to mind as we women went off to bed. There were moments of unity. After a fireworks concert on Hampstead Heath, my parents and I began a sing-song with the audience. Raphael, delighted, supplied the words for 'Maybe It's Because I'm a Londoner' and we grew sentimental over 'My Old Dutch'; even the taxi driver chipped in on the way home.

The Jewishness I fell in love with was in part a fabrication, though one that Raphael was happy to embroider with me. He told me Jewish jokes, which usually had no punchline, and which offered a safety valve for anti-Semitism, including one involving a rigmarole (the English would say 'a shaggy-dog story') about the resale of a wife's ring which goes the round of friends and relatives until one of them decides to keep it, and the original owner complains, 'But why? We were making such a good profit from it.' In his fifties, Raphael became more relaxed about his Jewish upbringing, though he did not, to my knowledge, ever purport to be, like Isaac Deutscher, a 'non-Jewish Jew', a secular left-wing internationalist who rejected Judaism but identified with a cultural Jewishness and acknowledged its influence on his thought. But I cannot know for sure and it is too late to ask him.

And my sense of Englishness? That became an object of interest. No longer taken for granted, it was something to think about, to work on. Imperceptibly my fieldwork among the middle classes shifted into exploring ideas of national identity, how they changed and who got to represent the English (these were the years when Mrs Thatcher was re-imagining and emphasizing an English, as opposed to British, national character). We found hilarious the notion that Raphael had married a phlegmatic Englishwoman with a stiff upper lip: 'Oy, has he got a wrong number!' our imaginary Jewish comic would say. Kissing the back of my hand and swearing his devotion, Raphael was always my beloved foreigner, but I felt enormously flattered when he told me that I had a Russian soul.

What is an 'identity'? Fixed stars do not govern a life. We both believed that the social relations we chose were as meaningful as those we inherited; that an origin was not a destiny; that an origin was not even an origin – scratch it, and another origin lies underneath. A person is a work in progress, always in the making, never made. And without the embrace of what is not us, how would we ever know who we are or who we might want to be?

7   Connubial

On the move – that's how I think of my time with Raphael. Always in motion. And yet a decade together is hardly the blink of an eye. It is as if the pages flick past so rapidly, like one of those early attempts at cinema, I see us running into the future, the courtship and the marriage flashing by at breakneck speed. In part it is an illusion, the effect of a premature ending, and of my longer life. I want memory to be a slowcoach. I want its shambling waywardness to side-step time.

True, I did a lot of shuttlecocking to and fro for the first few years, between London Bridge and Brighton, up at six in the morning, the metabolic rate of my life racing. And a state of emergency was always Raphael's default condition, a hangover, he reckoned, from being in the Party, when political activism meant a sense of permanent crisis. A favourite story of his: how the Victorian critic Thomas Carlyle would arrive feverish and slathered with sweat to give his lectures, having ridden a horse full pelt down Pall Mall. Raphael was always running to stations, jumping on trains, even if the wrong ones; taking taxis to squeeze out yet another drop of time for preparing teaching or correcting manuscripts. I got used to feeling like a small boat bobbing in the backwash, trying to find an even keel.

In Spitalfields my mental suitcase was always packed. I imagined we would move into an easier house; I could not see how a baby, if we had one, would 'fit' into Elder Street, how I would cope given the spiral stairs, the plumbing, and so on, though my neighbour, Lucinda, was cheerfully having her first child only a couple of doors down. I spent most of the marriage making space, clearing books and papers. By the time it had become a home, accommodating us both and fitting the new life we had made together, it was time to let go. Moving and making room were the leitmotifs of that marriage and of the mourning that followed.

If my life with Raphael is accelerating away from me, and this memoir seems a way of putting on the brakes, am I trying to master the art of losing, as the poet Elizabeth Bishop advises? The 'One Art', her poem calls it. Loss prompts her to write, and writing might even – is she kidding herself? – keep the disaster of it within bounds. Freud thought that children cope with love being taken away by re-enacting its absence compulsively on their own terms. And what are words, a poem or a memoir, if not signs of an absence? Transience, the precariousness of things, the paradox that not holding on too tight safeguards love: even Death, the ultimate disappearing act, can be turned to good use if you can learn, so the poets and the sages tell us, how to be a lodger in your life.

★

Married life. How did we live together? What changed? I passed my driving test and got a second-hand car, a Mini Metro with a faulty clutch but hardly any miles on the clock. Now I could reach Hampstead Heath for walks or drive hell for leather to the coast for a breather. Raphael would fall asleep in seconds, then wake with a start, and seize the wheel at roundabouts in case I had not noticed the other cars. On leave from the poly I took a course in massage at the Bethnal Green Buddhist Centre, thinking I could at least set up a sideline soothing the aching necks and backs of colleagues. What I really wanted was to leave my job and be in one place. Eventually I sold my share of the house in Brighton and used the small amount of profit to go freelance, reckoning I could pay myself about £700 a month for up to three years when the money would run out. Raphael was wary; I had published so little. At the party to say farewell, my colleagues gave me a large white wicker elephant. No one commented on the unconscious symbolism.

I would never have asked Raphael to support me. We never knew what the other earned, or what was in our bank balances, except in vague terms. It was certainly cheaper to live together in one house. Raphael had only a very small mortgage, taken out for the central heating I had insisted on. We kept a housekeeping book in which we listed sums for our shopping or other bills and totted it all up at the end of each month, paying each other any difference. We never had house insurance, a joint account or any savings to speak of. From Raphael I learnt not to pay any bill until the red demand appeared, because companies made interest on your cash. He never had a credit card. With my first I ran up hefty debts, but a timely book contract for my thesis came with the princely sum of £500. Taxis were Raphael's one extravagance; clothes and running the car were mine. Books were a necessity.

To begin with, Raphael did the lion's share of the housework, or rather I did, since lions do very little. But once I had moved in properly, cleaning and tidying – all the rituals of domesticity – were also a way of feeling at home. No doubt

we did the minimum by most people's standards: sweeping
or washing the kitchen floor and changing sheets and towels
fortnightly; a blitz with the hoover when friends were coming to stay; bathroom and toilet once a week. Raphael
preferred the labour-intensive. He vacuumed energetically,
no mean feat in a house with a narrow, twisting staircase
where he had to cantilever the hoover over five floors. A pol-
isher and special dubbin to buff the red quarry tiles in the
kitchen appeared on occasion, which meant moving the table
and other furniture, and Raphael stripping off like a navvy
for most of the day. He was equally enthusiastic at scrubbing
the bath or toilet, a task we took in turns. We rarely dusted,
except in the bedroom, because dust was our climate, the
house's environment. The books and papers in every room,
the open chimneys and the floorboards on every level, some
gappy and needing caulking, precipitated a continual seepage
of fine particles through the house.

My housewifery was learnt from my mother, whose own
skills came from hers. My grandmother had been in service
and frequently expressed her contempt for those who 'did not
know one end of a broom from the other'. I was surprised to
learn how many feminists, past and present, employed clean-
ers as a matter of course, never asking their menfolk to do
chores but happy to delegate their dirty work to other women.
Raphael boggled at my household lore: how to treat ink
stains with milk, or blood with salt; how to iron a shirt's col-
lar and cuffs first; how to dust or wipe a surface of crumbs so
that they gathered and fell into an open palm rather than on
the floor – your domestic culture, he called it. I liked to iron
after tea, listening to the radio, though Raphael never
expected or asked me to. These domestic habits connected me

to my past, to the days when as a small girl I helped my mother
turn hospital corners on the beds and felt important running
my duster over the furniture downstairs. When I thought of
her with a pile of ironing to get through on a Sunday evening, I was well aware how romantic my vision was.

Raphael and I also shared the cooking and shopping,
although he could never quite manage meals for two. Alone
he treated food as fuel, stoking up on takeaway chicken and
chips or on substantial lunches provided by Evelyn, the cook
at Ruskin. He always made a meal from scratch, usually
beginning when the guests arrived, pounding herbs vigor-
ously with a pestle and mortar, whisking the batter for
aubergine fritters, making the stuffing for red peppers. Guests
would be asked their views on the quality of the sauce or the
progress of the meal, which would usually appear around
9 p.m. I never got used to dinner parties, though these were
very casual, chafing at the performative element and wanting, of course, to shine. I was happier starting a tradition of
Christmas parties in Elder Street, baking mince pies and
sending out home-made cards with my photographs of the
district, our red-tiled rooftops loured over by the massive
bulk of Broadgate. Raphael concocted a bright-blue 'Spitalfields punch' from various spirits.

In time, of course, I saw Raphael more in the round and
was able to look after him. He was inordinately distressed by
breakages and by constantly losing his few personal items:
keys, diary, wallet, pens and especially spectacles (six times in
one week, my diary says). I impressed him with my ability to
sleuth them out by retracing his steps up and down the house.
Constitutionally unpunctual, he was truly alarmed by travel
and always running late. He hated getting from A to B, and

would go charging back to the house several times for a handkerchief, a book or a letter he wanted to post, or to make a quick call. We always arrived at the station with thirty seconds to spare and with me constantly chivvying him like a bad-tempered mother. I made a plan. We would meet at the barrier. Miraculously, he began leaving with me more or less on time. Did the desire not to be separated prove stronger than the desire to stay at home? Or could his 'Communist unconscious', as we called it, not allow such a blatant display of self-centredness?

When I read the novelist Olivia Manning's *Balkan Trilogy*, in which her husband, R. D. Smith, appears thinly disguised as the passionate Communist Guy Pringle, I thought I recognized many of Raphael's traits, the friendliness and generosity to others, but also the refusal to get angry, preferring to believe utterly in the power of argument. Both tendencies – the beguiling openness and the extreme rationalism – were partly tactical, derived perhaps from the Party strategy in the 1930s for a Popular Front, whereby everyone was to be treated as a potential recruit. It did not always go down well. Raphael's frank curiosity, his fervent talk, could annoy people. Once in an Oxford pub with his students, a drunk punched him on sight. Raphael, feeling sorry for him, gently asked why ('I don't like your face' might have been the conventional, irrational answer). About to get more of a thrashing, Raphael was hurried out of the firing line by his students. His serenity could be a blithe inability to tune in to others. After an evening out, he would marvel when I told him of the tensions I picked up between couples, the looks and asides, which he had entirely missed. He lacked, in his words, the right 'antennae'.

A kind of graceful formality, perhaps from being an only child among adults, came easily to him. Raphael's ideal was that we should always be courteous to each other, saying 'please' and 'thank you' for meals or for the performing of domestic chores. He would not quarrel with me. Sometimes it felt like a lack of acknowledgement or as if I were being patronized. I had grown up in a volatile family and watched white-faced from my corner of the kitchen table as the shouting escalated and the door slammed, and 'I hate you!' was hurled at my father as my sister flung herself out of the room. Raphael recalled how many men in his past political life had thrown their weight about; he winced at the arrogance of his own younger self. His breakdown, he said, had cured him of his temper. Nonetheless, his passive resistance could be just as intimidating. 'Who do you think you are – Jesus Christ?' I screamed one day when his patient argument infuriated me. I rushed into his study and tore up the manuscript on his desk, scattering the pieces on the floor. Whether consciously or not, my vandalism was half-hearted. I had ripped up a handwritten draft of which he had a typed copy.

Raphael enjoyed being uxorious, not telephoning his friend Gareth after eleven at night, for instance, 'for the sake of the marriage', as if it were a third person. He savoured our domestic habits but only once he had convinced himself that it was all somehow improvised. For my part, I saw the virtue in realizing that everything could be rearranged: a meal invented on the spot or left half eaten in a restaurant; a show or film abandoned halfway through; an appointment politely rescheduled; a holiday cancelled – nothing need be set in stone. Obligations were accepted because one wanted them. They were not traps. 'I am absolutely jammed up for the next three weeks,' he'd reply to a request from friends or colleagues, and somehow they never took offence.

All marriages are exchanges of gifts and needs, and we went on bartering. Raphael unbent a little towards Holly-wood film (we burnt a small turkey one Christmas as we sat upstairs engrossed by Frank Capra's *It's a Wonderful Life*) and he introduced me to classics of foreign cinema which were dear to his heart, *L'Atalante*, *Bicycle Thieves* and *Les Enfants du Paradis*. Together we pored over those English films whose culture was alien to both of us, the historical romances, say, from the Gainsborough Studios, with their cut-glass accents and emotional restraint. In Devon I persuaded him into Anglican churches for the first time and learnt the history of the Church of England's collusion with the enclosure of com-mon land while we examined the mason's marks. His puritan streak often took the form of disbelieving wonder – at room service, say, or the size of the beds on a brief trip to Con-necticut; and our holiday souvenirs frequently bore signs of a didactic impulse – the handmade tiles of peasants treading grapes from a tiny shop in Barcelona; from Italy, the carving of an old woman burdened by her fardels of twigs. Object les-sons in people's history, they were also beautiful in themselves. When Raphael hung a hand-coloured daguerreotype of a Brittany beach over his study mantelpiece, I took it as a small triumph for the pleasure principle.

I carried on home-making, improving. A new oven no longer charred my fingers along with the toast. Behind the old stove we found a mausoleum (a miceoleum?) of withered rodents chased there by the cat. A washbasin in the attic made life more civilized; and a red phone for the kitchen wall, the height, I thought, of urban chic, saved us from hectically dashing up flights of stairs. I bought a rust-coloured armchair for 'the room' upstairs and a velvet put-you-up to replace the bone-numbing futon; but, intransigent as it was, the house stood its ground and to the majority of visitors it appeared hardly changed at all.

In Spitalfields the wave of demolition and construction came ever nearer. When the developers set their sights on the fruit-and-veg market, a chorus joined in, including some of the market traders, agreeing it should go. Congested and impractical, it was also considered an eyesore by a number of locals, conservationists among them. For Raphael the market was the heart of the district, though not for romantic reasons. Incorporating and sustaining a variety of trades and industries for centuries, it protected the mixed character of the district and was a bulwark against 'office blight' with its homogenizing sterility and its haemorrhaging of residential life. Without the market's noise and messiness, he argued, international finance would dig in and property values would soar beyond the reach of local people, whether for homes or livelihoods. Ironically too, it was part of the 'pathos of conservation', as he called it, that the newly restored and more respectable Georgian houses increased the appeal of the district to the money-minded who so often came without any attachment to the area's history. The heritage innovations on our streets, 'Victorian-style' carriage lamps and fake bollards alongside the original cast-iron ones, were harbingers of the future. Together we debated, went to meetings and protested, and I got my first taste of the vitriol that was spewed out at council meetings, and of the relative helplessness of the council compared to the power that the biggest corporations could wield.

The market closed in 1991. In the next couple of years the IRA bombs brought their own destruction to the area but did little to halt the onslaught of redevelopment, though the NatWest tower, a different kind of eyesore, was badly hit. With Bishopsgate hushed and the City closed off, I went for a walk and watched as clouds of paper drifted down from the shattered buildings and were blown willy-nilly up the street.

★

Stops and starts. My break from teaching was a brief hibernation. Yet again the money ran out sooner than planned and I applied for a university lectureship, perhaps still trying to prove myself, still wanting to pass, as it were, the next exam. A couple of months into the new job I developed vertigo and lay in the attic with my head swirling, glimpsing out of the corner of my eye a little girl in nylon slacks, top and Pirelli slippers – myself as a child in the 1960s. I wrote some short fictional pieces and was pleased to find that I had so much past inside me. Nothing, it seemed, was lost. The experience led me into therapy at the Institute of Group Analysis. Established by Dr S. H. Foulkes, whose psychoanalytic work in the 1930s had brought him into close contact with the Frankfurt School of social theory (Max Horkheimer, Theodor W. Adorno and Herbert Marcuse were among its luminaries), it emphasized the social nature of being human, the relation between the individual and the group. I signed up for individual sessions.

Intellectual life, though, was far from solitary. Raphael and I continued to work and write together, organizing workshops, including two on the Conservative government's plans for a national curriculum, and outlining a co-authored book on the English stage between the wars, imagining many happy visits to London theatres. As part of the editorial collective of *Feminist Review*, an academic journal that had originated within sociology but reached across the humanities, I read the more literary submissions and the occasional wodge of poetry. More meetings in London kitchens, and, on my part at least, some anxiety as to whether I could knock up hummus and taramasalata as easily as they did. At the back of my mind was the idea of 'a Portsmouth book' about the working-class past, but I could not discuss it or imagine its form.

I needed to withdraw to write, preferring secrecy, but writing was always a sociable, public and accountable activity for Raphael. He consulted others at every stage, sometimes buttonholing them on the phone for hours (I vetoed his ambushing me until I had at least had my first cup of tea). A conversation turned into notes with a scrupulous acknowledgement; each note then morphed into a sentence, the sentence into a paragraph. Note-making was second nature to Raphael, a throwback to his days as a young Communist, but his method derived from that of the social investigators Sidney and Beatrice Webb, who perfected it for the 'scientific historian' in the 1880s and 1890s. Each thought or reference to a source was written or pasted on to a single side of a loose sheet of paper. It might be the source itself – an advertisement, a jam-jar label or an extract from a Xerox – it mattered only that it was attributed and sub-headed under a theme. Then the notes were filed in groups. Scholarly prestidigitation allowed the pages to be constantly reshuffled so that new combinations of ideas appeared, presuppositions might be overturned and surprising connections thereby generated. In theory too, someone else could pick up where you left off and rearrange your notes to suit their own research. All that was needed was reams of rough paper, scissors and a pot of glue, phalanxes of lever-arch files, and a hole puncher which liberally pointillized our floor with stray dots. The method suited Raphael, who was quite willing to dismantle his arguments and start again; no thought was ever comprehensive or complete, no argument final. As my work took a more historical turn, I too adopted this method and created – heaven help me! – my own rows of cumbersome ring binders.

Raphael distrusted the identity of 'writer' and saw little glamour in it. It was not enough of a *raison d'être*. The writing had to be *for* something – certainly for something more than advancing a career. With its overtones of solipsism and self-importance, he also knew how the idea of being a writer could wreck the lives of others. Bill, Minna's husband, wrote lyrics in the manner of Dylan Thomas but spent his life anguished at what he had not achieved. Raphael's approach was workmanlike: he needed to 'get up a head of steam' on an article, 'wrestle' with a paragraph and 'sweat it out'. His concentration was phenomenal. I met him once at the Aldwych Theatre in the Strand. He was squatting on the pavement, marking up proofs on his knees, utterly oblivious to the crowds milling around him, entertained or irritated. I was impressed but felt protective of him and a little embarrassed.

Although I was not a tyro, from Raphael I learnt how to hone my prose and to search over and again for the right word. Seeing his ferociously corrected scripts, I learnt to cut repetitions and avoid half echoes, to cut overlong sentences in two, to avoid too many lists, like this one. These were ideals, of course, to aspire to. Mostly I saw how everything could be improved by yet another combing through. I showed him everything I wrote, railing at every suggestion, however useful or helpful. He took to doing the same and welcomed every criticism. We learnt each other's tics and pointed out obscurities. Like Raphael, I began sending out my articles to friends, seeing every essay as just that – an attempt. Raphael, though, was a publisher's nightmare, unable to let go of anything. He would claw back a script at every stage, covering each proof with fresh alterations; smothered in deletions, additions and marginalia, his manuscripts could only be his.

Words, words, the power of words – always that perfect phrase just out of reach. Words were to persuade, cajole, convince; to make connections, make allies, a form of cooperation at best; and even at the worst an enemy's strong points must be acknowledged before weaknesses were pointed out. It was always worth trying to get it right, rewriting, rewriting, approximating to as much of the truth as possible. Writing was a way to practise fearlessness. When an office worker walked into a protruding branch of our bay tree, planted outside the house in a collapsing tea chest, she broke her spectacles. In an angry note she demanded compensation. Raphael replied to her with such courtesy and honesty – we were so *desperate* for green in our street, he wrote, and desperately sorry too – that she relented.

From Raphael I learnt how a book was put together: from the inching up of a paragraph to the finished piece sent off to the typesetter; the correcting of 'galleys' and proofs, with their arcane hieroglyphics, the printer's marks, all the processes of subediting and finalizing a text which were never usually explained to the uninitiated. I met editors, publishers, journalists, and I took it all in. (Raphael also had a hapless literary agent with whom he appeared to be constantly and politely at daggers drawn, but I never saw her.) A book was the work of many hands, editors no more and no less important than the much put-upon staff at the print shop near Liverpool Street, who laboured with him over the copying machine in a cramped, hot cubicle ripe with fumes. I approved of this attitude. My parents always talked to the postman or the woman working the till. They knew what it was like to be treated as invisible.

Part of Raphael's charm lay in his being entirely unabashed by others. On our first train journey back to Brighton he produced an enormous smelly French cheese to share with bread and a bottle of wine as if we were travelling through the Dordogne and not the outskirts of suburban Croydon. When the passenger opposite looked worried, he was instantly offered refreshment (and, being English, politely declined). Years later, giving a prestigious James Ford Lecture in history at Oxford University, Raphael avoided the flummery of a gown, turned up with an overflowing bag as usual and proceeded, as he always did, to pull books from it to back up his argument, like so many rabbits out of a hat. It was the Webbs' method as theatre, as if his thought was being improvised as he spoke, quite the opposite of the leaden reading of a lecture. If he cut a comical as well as an authoritative figure, he did not care. His subject was deadly serious, however, 'The Tory Interpretation of History'.

I never lost the thrill of finding manuscripts, proofs and booksellers' catalogues around the house, though I banished

the teetering piles from the spiral staircase, slippery enough
as it was without handholds for both of us to take a tumble
at least once a year. Nor were books ever quite tools to me.
As for many an autodidact and studious achiever, they
were precious and beloved companions. I tended to savour
what I read, while Raphael metaphorically 'gutted' books
or 'filleted' them, riffling through their pages as fast as he
could to make notes. He thought nothing of marking his
own books, though I would look askance. Our ways of
working remained stubbornly opposed. Raphael worked as
many hours as he could, skipping meals if I was not home. I
found I needed a rhythm and shape to the day and learnt to
establish it.

Raphael had a way of making what was current seem
strange, a sociology of the present which was always acute.
When the *New Statesman* published a couple of my memoir
pieces with my photograph appended, a relatively new custom, Raphael observed mildly that, probably, I wouldn't
want to be a columnist. It was a role he associated with 'the
yellow press', a journalism that relied too much on constant
opinion and too little on fact-based research. I was discon-
certed. 'Why do we need to know,' he asked pertinently,
'what a journalist looks like?' The culture of celebrity, with
its promotion of individual personality, was then in its infancy,
but I took the point. When *Forever England*, my first book, was
reviewed – my first ever 'notice', and in the national press to
boot – it was mostly laudatory but came with a sting in its
tail. I was devastated. Raphael, on the other hand, was over
the moon: 'The book is controversial! How marvellous!' he
cried. I suspected nonetheless that I had got 'an 'ology'.

At our desks in Elder Street in 1992.

★

How to summarize a marriage? The human body, apparently, renews itself every seven years, sloughing off cells like a snakeskin. Married life, perhaps, must renew itself too, take on another life every seven years or so. A marriage is many marriages, made and remade serially, if we are lucky, and able to evolve, after that first itch to be rid of the old skin. Change *will* come, whether we want it or not. Children are born, or not born; they come and go. We grow older; our parents die – these are the most obvious prompts. But a married life has its internal logic too: the fascinating, desirable strangeness (desirable because strange) of the other person becomes familiar and annoying. What then? The Lawrentian passion subsides. What then? I think it must be the hardest thing on earth to live with another human being, to share a life, and to bear in mind, *really* bear in mind, that this person is different. Is not you. And as the years go on, how easily this is forgotten.

Raphael and I never had those years. Ours was, to some extent, a perpetual romance and a perpetual disenchantment, with no children to threaten its intimacy. But I have always craved this one-to-one knowledge of another person and only latterly, in my middle age, found groups and being in groups an equally enticing source of knowledge. We emerged, Raphael and I, from the melting-pot stage of meeting; perhaps he emerged rather sooner than I since he had more scaffolding from a longer, older life. *I* emerged, then, and found myself after several years no longer so ill at ease or so much an outsider. I felt less of, *was* less of, an impostor. Time had worked its magic. I *was* writing; Raphael's friends were used to me; several liked me and sought me out; and we were a married couple now, a given, a known quantity.

I was older, of course, nearly forty. No longer so girlish-looking. I grew my hair and curled it, then straightened it again; I put on weight, then lost it, then put it on again and became more matronly, as if I wanted to be of more consequence. But after seven years I was a fait accompli. Invitations now came to both of us and my name was spelt right. We never quite had the life of the couple pottering around the house, listening to the radio or making meals together; we never bickered either. Yet Raphael was essential to my feeling of home. Family gatherings and visits on both sides felt more chosen, less compelled – but oh, the deep contentedness of eschewing them altogether and going to my books on a Christmas Day with no one disapproving.

What would have come next? What skins might we have grown or shed? Another seven years, say, would have taken Raphael towards his seventies and me through menopause. Would I have stayed faithful, as younger partners so often don't? I imagine so because infidelity has always struck me as degrading and I have a lot of pride. I would not like to be seen to behave badly. And another seven? Would I have written more or less? Would it have mattered?

And Raphael. He had become connubial. He no longer camped out on his study floor but elected to come to bed with me by eleven. He no longer broke his sleep and mine several times a night. He got up early – fourish, fiveish – napping a little at his desk before feeding the cat, who often slept aslant his papers, and brought me a cup of tea. He took more holidays and breaks and I took more writing to do on those holidays, dissolving the distinction; and he finally stopped smoking. Not from fear of death, at least not consciously, he said, but from vanity. When he found himself wheezing and hacking after his usual gallop to Liverpool Street, loaded up with the canvas rucksack of books, he stopped. Cold turkey. Straight off. And never went back.

I like to think our edges softened; his old comrade Stuart Hall wrote in his obituary that Raphael 'mellowed'. I think I became more defined. I grew up a bit, I suppose. Raphael missed some of his old life, certainly. He missed the endlessly sociable evenings, the cooking for seven or twelve, and might voice this longing wistfully now and then. Something had to give. Intimacy comes at a cost. My own life was more crowded, fuller than ever; his had contracted a little. In his sixtieth year he put together *Theatres of Memory*, his first single-authored volume. 'But in nineteenth-century Oxford, darling,' he said, tickled by the thought, 'a gentleman would aim to publish posthumously.'

One year, as part of my campaign for more shared pleasures, Raphael and I took a package holiday to Minorca and a group boat trip around the coast near Mahon. As we sailed into the bay where we were to have a paella lunch on the beach, we were invited to dive into the sparkling water and swim to the shore, or wait till we had anchored nearer and wade over. I am a strong swimmer but I have never liked to dive, so I watched the more confident climb on to the bows. Suddenly there was Raphael, teetering on the edge, then just as suddenly – gone. I thought he could not swim. So I followed. Thanks to a mixture of improvised doggy paddle and quickly getting into his depth, he made it, breathless and unharmed, to the sand. What on earth had prompted him to leap – sheer willpower, impatience or the desire to join in? Or something else entirely? He could not say. He had acted on impulse and I too hadn't thought twice.

Much later he remembered: his father had taught him a few strokes in their holidays together at Port Isaac in Cornwall. The swimming, with this memory of his father, had surfaced only with our holidays in the sun, so perhaps the plunge was for him into some other element, some other self. I will never know. But I see now that he trusted me too. We were saving each other, as lovers must, from our demons; we would not let the other drown.

8 Appassionata

I dread rehearsing the antediluvian days, the days before the flood, when I seem, with the tenderness of hindsight, touchingly innocent. And yet the metaphor is wrong. There was no watershed, no sudden dramatic shift, only the same emotions surfacing again and again in the months to come, not in sequence but at random – disbelief, fury, guilt, hopefulness, despair, relief (not to mention tetchiness, peevishness, self-pity). My emotions, not Raphael's.

My diary goes on, as diaries do, onwards and upwards. I'm 'quids in', I write in the spring of 1995, finally offered a part-time lecturing arrangement in London to suit me. Raphael's own life is 'flourishing': 'rave reviews' for *Theatres of Memory*. We are 'like an old married couple' and I'm suddenly taken over by 'Nelly', the idea for a book about Virginia Woolf and her servants, a seed grown from reading Woolf's diaries years before, and which will wait another ten years for fruition. I am full of plans. I shall finish therapy, go on holiday for some spring sun or buy a cottage in Suffolk (that old chestnut) and be a writer – 'or at least half a one by the time I'm forty'. Why should it seem worse, looking back, that life was so full? It would hardly have been better if we had been miserable.

No matter how many times I give the game away, Raphael's death is the climax of this memoir. But that was not how we lived in the stream of life, its comings and goings, or in what we call 'society' or 'history'. Friends fell in love in those years, had children; others died; governments came and went; laws were passed and wars waged; and then there was the dailiness, the so-called uneventfulness, the *stuff* of life – so little of it recorded, despite my garrulous journals. It all washes over us, leaving a few tidemarks in the sand.

And yet we did live differently after Raphael's cancer was diagnosed. We carried on with our tasks, our friendships and work but, like others faced with the question of life and death, we could also be translated on to a more absolute plane, which freed us from the mundane and the taken for granted. Time passed; we went to our appointments, to our desks, to the cinema or the theatre, the shops. And time stood still, was concentrated and intensified, sometimes exalted. 'So much sweetness,' I wrote in my diary during the worst of times, by which I meant love.

No one except a saint or guru can live their lives *sub specie aeternitatis*, in a continual dialogue with existence and mortality. But we had our moments. 'I am improvising from day to day,' I wrote with a sense of achievement while Raphael made new plans for the future and our roles were temporarily reversed. And death, when it came, was not a summing up, though it was tempting to make it so. It was a fact.

★

We spent the Christmas of 1994 in Cornwall, in a rented cottage in Gorran Haven on the Roseland Peninsula. Its ground floor was a cellar for fishing boats and their tackle, while the first-floor sitting room was hard up against the small beach and the incoming waves. The beach was sunless by lunchtime and therefore empty. Trippers went elsewhere and we walked in peace on the stones or clambered up the paths. On Christmas Eve we collected our turkey, baked at the village shop, and trundled it home, still hot, in a wheelbarrow. Raphael had complained for a while of an ache in his chest which the doctor reckoned was a pulled muscle, perhaps from hoisting the overloaded army rucksack. We made a special trip to the chemist at Polperro to get more painkillers.

About his body Raphael was both very private and, like many men, largely indifferent. Health was a matter of oblivion and he was rarely ill: one or two colds, never flu; a passing sore throat. Any other afflictions he kept to himself, took paracetamol and worked, falling asleep at his desk if need be. Not once did he take to his bed. Pyjamas and a dressing gown, which I had given him, were special outfits, to be taken down to my parents' house in Portsmouth, where they were de rigueur. Having to resort to a robe, later in the illness, made him feel, he said, like Oblomov, the eponymous hero of the novel by Ivan Goncharov who lounges about all day, barely moving between his chair and his bed.

Throughout his treatment he spoke of his body as if it bore some novel, possibly unknown, relation to himself. He referred to his limbs with the definite article – 'the leg' or 'the arm' – as if saying 'my' was too much admission of ownership. He never appeared to be personally ashamed or feel degraded by the indignities the cancer inflicted on him; he would tell the GP of my ministrations proudly and without embarrassment. This impersonality helped him too, I think, to resist the bombardment of details about his condition. These interested him only in so far as he might get on with his life. Anatomy and biology were complete blind spots in his knowledge. He never read the 'how to cope with' booklets handed to him, rapidly setting aside the notes we made in the consultations.

I am reminded of a walk we once took around the bay near Minehead in Somerset. Up on the cliffs we could see the town in the distance a few miles away. Those miles magically extended themselves the further we walked in their direction. It came on to rain. We had nothing much by way of snacks to keep us going, and eventually, with the light failing, we had to turn back. But up until that last minute Raphael had wanted to go on, remained cheerful and undaunted, as I grew more irritable.

So it was in illness. He made no concessions to the disease until he had to. When he could no longer turn the key in the front door and push it open – his wrists too spindly – he simply stayed in; when he could not manage the stairs, he had a bed and a desk brought up to the first floor and dug in there; when he could no longer swallow, he chose to stop eating. But not before time, not an inch to be given to that ultimate adversary, who will, you can be sure of it, always take a mile.

'I shan't make you a widow this year,' he announced airily, as we made our way to a New Year's Eve party to herald 1996. And I believed him. His faith was contagious. When he was very sick, he asked me to read to him 'some lines', first Thomas Hardy, and then T. S. Eliot's 'Prufrock': I tried foisting some of *Four Quartets* upon him, with all the ruthlessness of nurses, but he preferred the self-deprecating human voice, having no use for Eliot's metaphysics.

★

Raphael's egalitarianism stood him in good stead. He soon called consultants by their first names and got on easy terms with them. They were a rum lot. We went from hospital to hospital in search of a diagnosis: was it a rare breast cancer? A secondary tumour from the skin or kidney? A sweat gland? A lung cancer but not from smoking? Even tuberculosis was canvassed in the course of nearly two years. First, the suave consultant at the Royal London, a Supreme Being of the old school, rubbing his hands together and breezing into the wards in a lordly fashion. Raphael told him of his involvement in a TV series that was in the pipeline. It was to be about Britain at the millennium and accompanied by a series of illustrated books like the handsome Shell Guides for motorists produced after the war. 'Don't make any plans,' the brute said, and foolishly we cancelled a holiday. At St Bartholomew's, near Smithfield, we were greeted by a fellow who seemed annoyed that I was there. He compared the new round of powerful antibiotics to the household cleaner Domestos. At the Royal Marsden, getting another second opinion, we were in and out in minutes. 'Not the case for me' was the brisk dismissal from the surgeon, whose striking head of hyacinthine curls, surely a perm, made him seem subtly untrustworthy.

The cancer went through its stages as cancer does. At first Raphael feels 'fit as a fiddle' and we both doubt the initial biopsies. But something is still out of joint. Raphael tells me he would rather be 'in a cloud of unknowing' if it weren't for the pain in his chest. He has, he says, 'no future imagination' and I have nothing but. 'It is human,' I reassure my diary, 'to feel afraid of letting him down, of not being able to cope.' But a day later, waiting for further test results, I find 'it just isn't possible to think of death all the time'. We spend our Sunday before Easter strolling along the Thames. 'At peace. A loving, funny time.'

We needed our dreams. At different times we both dreamt that the house was on fire. I had strange scrabbling night-mares of rats or mice scurrying over my pillow. We took a package holiday to Bellagio on Lake Como. The hotel gave us a dank, squalid room. A fetid odour of drains or worse pervaded it and there was barely space for what was barely a double bed. On our first night I dreamt that we were sunbath-ing on an Australian beach, lying as if still in bed in each other's arms. Coming towards us was a huge, towering wave, a tsunami, though I wouldn't have known that word then, about to engulf us. We were paralysed and I heard someone say – an Australian – 'They're finished.' Next morning Raphael requested another room, complaining, 'I can't even make love to my wife,' a successful appeal to Italian passions.

That holiday, our last, was not a success. The town, with its magnificent lake, felt too shut in; the steps were too steep; we could not 'get away'. In a shop full of chic clothing, Raphael bought a stylish blouson in dark blue suede with a green lea-ther reversible lining. At £450 it was an unheard-of luxury, an offering of sorts to gods that we didn't believe in and a 'prophylactic', as Raphael put it, 'against death'. And who is to say that it didn't keep the Reaper off a little longer? Raphael made a will not long before we left, but both of us, uncharacteristically, opened savings accounts. Banking on a future?

In 1996 Raphael had taught full-time at Ruskin College for nearly thirty-two years. When the University of East London invited him to set up a London History Centre, he was galvanized by the prospect of a fresh start. Overflowing with possibilities for collaborative work, he outlined a millennium project on 'The Exploding Metropolis: London and Its Regions 1919–39', and a series of 'East London Papers', or pamphlets, under multiple authorship. Among the proposed titles were 'Brick Lane: East London's Dhaka 1960–1997'; 'The East End Jewish Wedding', a study which 'might provoke others by London Greeks, Turks, Kurds, Italians, Irish' ('It could run for ever,' he noted); and 'The History of the East End Dog', from their presence in the weavers' sports of the 1820s to their contemporary role as companions of the homeless. The university agreed to his having a central office. We set him up in a basement room in the Bishopsgate Institute, opposite Liverpool Street station, where he often worked, a mere five minutes away from home; his aunt Sarah donated a modernist rug and I manhandled it down the stairs. Raphael was delighted with the troglodyte darkness and the chance to rely on the immense enthusiasm and encyclopaedic knowledge of the Bishopsgate's chief librarian, David Webb.

We decided not to give out constant updates on the illness. The cancer, in his view, was not interesting to talk about, nor were the vicissitudes of his physical state. When he gave lectures to over a hundred students during some chemotherapy, he 'had a little retch afterwards', he told me, but thought no one took much notice. There were some comic subterfuges, like staging a PhD viva in our front room, the coffee cups laid out in advance and Raphael barely moving from his chair, secretly lined with a sheepskin to help him sit comfortably, as I admitted our guests. In part the embargo was to spare me the role of messenger, living a more and more second-hand existence as his mouthpiece; in part too, such conversations were for him a kind of nadir, a species of moaning, wasting precious time, anathema still to the young Communist within him and perhaps to his generation; he was too old to 'let it all hang out'.

I, on the other hand, needed to talk. I continued my psychotherapy at the Institute of Group Analysis and the sessions became weekly, blessed Thursday hours where I could pour out tears and words or immerse myself in a silence of my own making. Nothing was taboo and I was centre stage. I kept my sessions going up to three days before Raphael died. They got me out of the house; they gave me a way of making sense. Sometimes I'd tell Raphael what had 'come up'. He got the benefit of it, he would say, like wrapping up warm.

Into a turquoise box file (a peacock among all the drab lever-arch files), which we called 'the cancer box', disappeared all the depressing hospital bumf and all our discontents: the chaos of misdiagnoses, or that final scan when the radiographer treated him like meat on a slab, ignoring his protests (I wrote to complain to the hospital, though I got no reply). More often the box testified to all the small kindnesses we encountered, the myriad reminders of the human touch: those nurses who patiently, time and again, sought out recalcitrant and obscure veins for their needles, stroking and patting and reassuring; or the driver of the black cab who took us to a final X-ray session and all but lifted Raphael, cradling him, over the threshold of the taxi and into the hospital foyer; and of the increasing attentiveness of physicians who could no longer hope to heal. The most knowledgeable admitted their limits. At University College Hospital, Raphael quizzed Professor Robert Souhami – 'Bob' – the most humane of men, about whether he would be able to give an inaugural lecture in

February 1997. They squared up to each other. 'I don't know, I honestly don't know,' the doctor replied.

*

In the autumn of 1996 I took unpaid leave from my post and tried to write a review or two but finished nothing. It was more important to have work to return to; I could not manage endings. Raphael and I did not talk much about death and thought it rather bad manners when others did. The reality of our situation was obvious enough without 'erecting finger-posts in conversation', as Henry James puts it in the scene between Isabel Archer and her dying cousin, Ralph, in *The Portrait of a Lady*. I took my cue from Raphael. But what went on inside him, I don't know, except for what he called his Jewish passivity prompting the occasional gloom when the outlook worsened with each test. Raphael's way of fighting was to get back to his desk and to do what he always did. To be in the present. The idea of a bucket list – what is that if not a sign of a frustrated life? Raphael was one of the lucky ones.

I also took this blessing from the illness: it untethered me (as my own cancer was to do many years later); it let me off the hook of obligations. Raphael was already used to a wife who spent the day in a dressing gown, in and out of bed, with her books and diary propped up, and now he sometimes took a nap alongside me. 'This is bliss,' I wrote in my diary, 'me chewing gum and Raphael asleep, naked, warm and bony. I wish I could bottle it up and dab it behind my ears and on my wrists.' As time went on, though, we led a more routinized life, starting the day together, with me doing the bulk of the shopping and cooking. Later, when the stairs proved too much, I would bring breakfast for us both up to the first-floor room where we set up a bed, and we'd watch some TV. Ironically there was now time to be idle together. Be careful what you wish for.

Of course I imagined being a widow ('Have you thought what you will do after?' the district nurse put it delicately). In fantasy such thoughts were painless and I seemed glamorous to myself: a young widow with a house in central London. They rose up involuntarily and I tried not to squash them; they offset the panic. I made some wild stabs at futurity. Should we try to have a child? But Raphael appreciated, he said, having *all* my love and attention. I know that a few years later, when my father was mortally ill, he and my mother agreed that she would leave their flat after his death and move to Somerset to live near my sister. It gave my father comfort to know this, he said, as if he were still looking after her. But Dad was eighty-one, not sixty-one. How could Raphael have borne to leave me? What meagre consolation would such planning give him or me?

Raphael's mother was waiting for a hip operation. We talked of spending Christmas with her and Raphael fended off her anxious phone calls. My own mother was far more insistent. Where she came from, where *I* came from, mothers and daughters were helpmeets, they shared calamities and they treated physical ailments as a staple of conversation; they moaned about their men, those blundering, violent or harmless creatures who knew so little about what mattered and were relegated to earning a living. The business of birth and death was women's work, once the blip of marriage, absorbing a stranger into the tribe, was over. She felt excluded, hurt, wanting to look after me, offering to come up. But Raphael did not want to be mothered by her, and I needed to be his wife and not her child. I needed all my energies to look after him. I was my mother's daughter all the same when I laid Raphael out, washed him and combed his hair, though I had long left that other country, her country, far behind.

In the last month or so, when Raphael could no longer leave the house and was finding writing arduous, I decided to interview him. As oral history it was a failure. Raphael was keen on my speaking as much as he did and on the tape we interrupt each other freely, calling each other 'darling', hardly the model of professionalism. I began conventionally enough with childhood memories, as if we had all the time in the world to work our leisurely way towards young adulthood and later life. Raphael recalled the fun of his holidays with his Welsh family, eating fish and chips at Porthcawl with his father; riding out in a black car with his uncle Ben, a doctor, visiting the miners in the valleys. Like a reverse Scheherazade, I tried to keep Raphael talking as he started to fade.

In our last session his voice on the tape has silted up and is barely audible; much of the recording is a furry hum, signifying the long pauses he took for naps. A black comedy sets in as Raphael repeats himself about materialism and how at Long Dene, the progressive (not left-wing) school he was sent to aged seven, the headmaster, Johnny, insisted that scientific agriculture was ruining British farming. We – Communists, he says over and over – were on the side of the machine. After his death I put the tapes away. Twenty years later, when I listen to them for the first time for this memoir I realize that Raphael's voice on the tape is a travesty. I transcribe the tapes. Then I throw them away.

★

And I have to turn the pages after all. Who would have thought that it would still be so hard after all these years? How the dead survive! I flinch at the details in my diary as if Raphael were still suffering and as if to write about it now exposes him as it might have done then. To what? What harm can come to him now? I wake up with a heavy heart and sob in John's arms. The wretched fact of surviving, and still, the relief. Being comforted by one husband for the loss of another. My own good luck. Oh, humanity! What rare and strange and loving creatures we are! Given half a chance.

That diary – such a mixed blessing. As if by turning all the pain into words I could escape its effects, the sacred distance of sheer vocabulary, chosen or intuited, the arm's length of the pen. But the diary *did* save me. It *was* a breathing space. It gave me something to do in the wards, in the exhausted after-noons, and in the phases of elation that followed any hopeful sign. It tolerated all my crazinesses: the day I turned to the Tarot and drew 'Death' first from the pack; my immersion in reading Jung, and the Jungian dreams which sprang like Cad-mus's teeth overnight, a cobra thrown into the room that roared like a tiger, I remember – all those bargains and wagers that I knew to be magical thinking and which saw me through the day, and then the hour.

I was writing my diary at Raphael's bedside not long before he died. Observing, recording, reflecting, but not for poster-ity. For me. In the name of understanding what cannot *be* understood. Dissolution. A person there – then gone.

I watched and recorded my sorrow, my anger, my guilty fantasies – oh, the longing for sex! – my recriminations, all my measly whining or bloated and grandiose needs and desires saying 'Me, me, me!' I noted how repulsive the world was; how I hated others, blithely healthy in their puny world. And those miracles of alchemy, those accesses of sheer love that daily came over and drew us ever closer. The diary was a companion as nothing else or no one else could be. Writing made it possible to say less to family and friends, as Raphael wanted. To keep more to ourselves. And a diary never ends.

★

Those last days. A rushed trip to Liverpool Street station to buy Häagen-Dazs ice cream, something Raphael could swallow with morphine crushed in it; we joked about his newly decadent tastes, and about Ellen, the softly spoken nurse sent by Marie Curie cancer care, a gentle Irishwoman who sat with him from ten till four, chatting interminably, much to Raphael's horror. She lasted one day. I bought an electric bell for Raphael to ring, as I slept two floors up in the attic, not realizing that the drug would so agitate and disorientate him that he would ring at random, fetching me up and down, with an imperious, often pointless summons. One day I offered – too soon, too soon – to sleep downstairs in his room: 'You've crossed the line,' he cried in a rare outburst at my confusing care with infantilizing.

We never said out loud that he wanted to die at home, but that was within my powers. I was forty – youngish, fittish. I could, just, take the sleepless nights, the nursing, lifting, bed-making, fetching and carrying, the physical load. But not the housework. For the first and last time in my life I employed a cleaner, Mick Pedroli, the housekeeper for our neighbour, Dennis Severs. He did a morning a week, polishing and scrubbing to the high standards of his Dutch upbringing and way beyond our own. Raphael barely touched the dishes friends brought for us to eat, but he left glowing tributes to the pears or casseroles on answering machines around London.

It was all I could do to be there and to be as much a fellow traveller as it was possible to be. Not to look away. I wanted to know and to use my intelligence, however limited or futile; I learnt the facts, listened to the doctors, filed away the sheaves of papers. In the medical section of Dillons, the university bookshop, I looked up 'cavitation' and 'cytology'. I was the archivist and this was my work. I hoped it would leave Raphael freer. If he wanted to say little about his feelings, that did not matter. I could guess.

I can attest, however, that being present, being a fellow traveller, did not soften any blows. My feelings were usually deferred until I was alone – such was the sense of emergency and then euphoria – until I was able to register on my senses what I had seen, but no physical suffering that I have personally undergone so far in life compares to being that witness. Nothing has been as agonizing as being a spectator, helpless, useless, unable to assuage suffering beyond the temporary solace of a drug or a drink, a wiping of the mouth and brow.

Over the intervening years I sometimes wondered if I took on more than I could manage. Not physically, though that did take its toll and erupt later in various aches and pains. But psychologically. 'You won't bear more than you can bear,' our friend Sally said to me cryptically. She reckoned my mind would simply shut off when the pain was approaching the unbearable. I think it did, and this, as I understand it, is a compassionate denial. But it opened up again far sooner than I expected, almost as soon as Raphael died. I tormented myself with all I had not done for him that I could have done, silly little momentous things – turning off the main light on that last evening when my eyes were tired and I wanted to rest, and he had wanted it left on. It proved in retrospect that I was a monster. I wanted to survive. 'Is there anything I can do for you?' I'd ask most days, and Raphael would often reply, 'You've done absolutely everything you can, darling.' Which was not true. I wasn't saving him. I couldn't keep him from dying. Freud sees these reproaches as part of the warding off of terror, the fear of death, of our own death, and fury at the other's dying.

'Not being able to bear more than you can bear', a refusal which is not conscious. No one in their right mind (and I mean this) can accept the reality of a loved one's imminent death. There is no acceptance, not in advance. Of course there were plenty of times when I wanted Raphael to die. I knew this was to be expected, even 'healthy'. I wanted to be free of the shadow cast over our lives, the endless trips to the hospital, the horrible sights, the uncertainty – if only he could die without actually dying! Or, the most feeble 'if only' of all, if only we could turn back time.

What I kept for myself, what I harboured and pondered in my heart, for years afterwards, was the horror of Raphael's dying. The seeing it, the being there, the *knowing*. I mean the horror of his *actually* dying, which no narrative can put into words. After nearly two years of illness we never thought it would happen. Not even when he could barely stand and hardly eat. It came as a shock, I swear. He died.

I don't think this is unusual and I don't think that for a thing to be known it has to be spoken of. We knew and we did not know. We lived with the doctors, the treatments, the loss of strength and all that entailed. We lived, that was the point, finding ways to think and work and observe; to have conversations: not to defend ourselves against death – no one has the power to do that – but to refuse to pre-empt it. But 'we' were not a 'we'. If I were to hazard at Raphael's stance, it was one, not of 'denial', but of resistance.

*

Raphael was so thoroughly dead. And the kind of death he had, at home, alone with me holding his hand, and without any medical interference or paraphernalia, I now see as a wonder. He had painkillers and regular visits from the local GP and a district nurse who changed the dressing on his chest, he had all the benefits of a free National Health Service; but in the end there was little by way of intervention. On the last Sunday my brother, Chris, drove up from Portsmouth to make an unplanned visit, arriving at about nine, much to Raphael's delight; my oldest friend, Fran, came to help me get more sleep; and Sally, too, arrived, the only other person Raphael said he could stand to look after him ('Ah, the two women I love most in the world,' he flirted as we supported him across the room). A nurse looked in briefly. Raphael surprised us by dying that night. So much so that in those early hours of Monday morning the locum who certificated the death raised the spectre of a post-mortem. I could hardly say to this total stranger that Raphael had been so alive that day I would never have dreamt of killing him.

I don't mean he was sprightly. In the early hours we had watched a Tory Party broadcast, something he had never done: 'Now I feel thoroughly miserable,' he said in a satisfied tone, as if his brain needed to be at one with his body. Listening to music, he chose not Bach but Beethoven's 'Appassionata', needing to be roused, not soothed. The drugs and weakness made him a little lachrymose, even schmaltzy, though he was always easily moved. 'They can't take the purity of our romance away, darling, can they?' he said to me, though it was not really a question. 'No,' I agreed, without knowing who 'they' were.

The post-mortem was quickly pooh-poohed by our usual doctor, who knew Raphael's frail condition. Why hadn't we called *him*? he asked. He could have saved me that distress. I heard in his voice a longing. He had wanted to see Raphael one more time and be entrusted with that last act.

Few people in British society have the luxury of sitting with their dead calmly and alone, if they wish, for as long as they like, until the wheels of officialdom grind into motion and what remains of the person becomes a body to be taken by strangers. Perhaps I sat for ten minutes before the locum was called, perhaps for half an hour. I know that I woke Sally and Fran and they joined me in a miniature wake at Raphael's side, with a tot or two of whiskey. After the doctor came, they went back to sleep or tried to. I stayed up. I sat with Raphael. I knew he was dead. At some point I lay down with him. I smelt his hair. I found it much harder than I expected it would be to close his eyelids, but that strange alchemy others have recorded, whereby a freshness returns to the face with the relaxing of muscles, and a youthful serenity suffuses the features – I saw that transformation. Beautiful as ever, my beloved; beautiful. I opened the window a little in a nod to a folk tradition and felt Raphael would approve. Out went his spirit, out into the dawn air.

★

I think it was a good death. Not because Raphael was surrounded by family and friends on his deathbed, medieval fashion, though a steady flow of visitors came to the house. One afternoon his cousins Yasha and Jenny stood proxy for the older generation and sat recalling the songs sung after the Passover meal when they were children, songs with nonsense endings, and much shouting and banging of the table: 'Haydl, didl, dam!' It was a good death because we made something of it together and he went on thinking and working. To be alive until you die, to achieve your own death and not have it dictated to you by medicine or convention, that is something – if not 'good', then good enough. Under the circumstances. Which were appalling. To die at nearly sixty-two is not to die young. But it is to die before your time, if only missing out on those mythical three score years and ten. Another eight seems little to have asked.

I needed to believe in the good death, of course. I thought it a 'Bolshevik' death, and included the word in the few lines for the newspaper, a romantic though not an entirely foolish gesture. I was remembering the salute that Raphael made me when I left Elder Street after my first night there. He raised a clenched fist and said in French to my startled delight, 'Courage!' by way of a comradely farewell. I forgot to put the date in the death notice. Some part of me, perhaps, could not bear to record it, to let it become history.

PART THREE

Mourning

9   Time out of Time

Formlessness is a condition of mourning. In January 1997 I went to see a Howard Hodgkin exhibition at the Hayward Gallery. I stood before an oil painting called *Lovers* in an ecstasy, dazed by the red and green swathes of bright, primal colour swooping like a rainbow and running right off the canvas, spilling over the black frame. A dialectical union of opposites, it evoked that dissolution of boundaries, the falling in love which mourning restages. Like love, grief stops history in its tracks; it has duration without narrative. For the lover, time concertinas into unbearably fleeting moments; for the mourner, each minute is monumental.

Like other fledgling mourners, all my efforts went into projection, into being with the deceased, taking off with them: wanting, in fact, to die. The sobbing, the dry heaving and violent racking of the body, the 'dissolving' into tears, all make the physical separation between the living and the dead seem less hard and fast. Those early months of mourning were, as we say, a blur. But mourning works against the will, by compulsive repetition. Eventually the repeated repetitions, all those anniversaries counted in days, then weeks, then months and years, force one to register that the absence feels different, if only by being, like the pain, more familiar. However stymied the mourner feels inside, however inert, outside changes remorselessly. So, for example, the general election that May was a terrible wrench, an assault on my inwardness.

Mourning reverses the speed of falling in love, prising apart the lover and the beloved.

Mourning is love's negative, proof that it has once been there; but it seems in excess of the original, seeping and leaking over the edges of the print. I can barely read my diaries from this period. They are so freighted with sheer unadulterated time, time that has to be weathered, that misbehaves like a sinister and comic surrealist clock, elongating, warping and folding. Nine in the morning. I'd check the time after what felt like another hour or two of blankness: still nine o'clock. A whole day to be waded through. 'I cried for an hour,' I wrote without exaggeration. My state was normal, though it felt, as all grief must and is, exceptional. Mourners, like lovers, are solipsists but the self is disintegrating, disorganized.

Yet I was lucky. The world was always there: the world I hated – dreary, smug and ignorant, with its stupid Christmas cards a week after the funeral, its misjudged telephone messages, its post addressed to the already dead; its clichés of sympathy, its unwanted advice, its fear and shying away (to the colleague who crossed over a college courtyard and hid: 'I saw you! I saw you!'). And that same world, so patient, so kind, a solid phalanx of friends, inviting me out, offering to come and stay; the friends who bore with me, whom I rang at all hours. Those who listened and did not interrupt, who said what I did not want to hear, and what I did. I have to read between the lines of my diaries to realize how much I was borne up by others. Even in those bleak pages sometimes gratitude breaks through the pall of grief, illuminating it like a kind of grace.

★

From the distance of twenty years I can see that in the first days and months of mourning I improvised an amalgam of old and new, a 'bricolage' of rituals and obsequies, of what passed for customary and what was new or imported. Much of what I did with Raphael's body – thumb-shutting his eyes, laying him out, holding a mini wake – came indirectly from my childhood, including the whisperings about the Roman Catholic Irish in our street. Whiskey seemed right, but who told me about keeping the curtains closed after opening a window for the dead? (I was inconsistent in my folk wisdom: I left the mirrors uncovered.) It was not, by any standards, conventional to stay alone with Raphael until the warmth left him; lying by him, talking to him, putting his wedding ring back on his finger, now that he no longer need worry about it slipping off.

I knew I would have to share mourning and I wanted to do right by Raphael, to do what was fitting, and give him a good send-off. At forty-one I had no experience of organizing a funeral; my parents were still alive. I had to feel my way. Highgate had been mentioned briefly about a year before when we made Raphael's will, almost as an afterthought. Raphael had no desire to discuss his death but was amused to learn, after I had rung them, that a grave at Highgate Cemetery could have room for two. We made macabre jokes about its connubiality. As a Marxist and a materialist he could not, he said, believe in the afterlife. Funerals, like birthday parties, are for other people. Both Raphael and I blenched at the idea of his having a hand in it, orchestrating perhaps one of those relentlessly cheerful humanist funerals we had attended where everyone remained dry-eyed. Nevertheless, cremation, the radical, progressive or freethinking option, which had its roots in Jacobinism, was never raised. The local Co-operative Funeral Services was an obvious choice.

Raphael saw Highgate Cemetery as a wonderful repository of Londoners. It was sited in an area he knew well and where his aunts and uncles and cousins still lived. One of his homes had been nearby in Croftdown Road and as a teenager he had cycled across the Heath to school, always late, he told me, on his bike bought from Chamberlayne's on the Kentish Town Road. He spoke animatedly of the theatre people buried there – the comedian Max Wall among them – but said nothing to me about political or personal connections with the place. I learnt years later that Dennis Butt was buried there. A Yorkshire wool-sorter and a rare adult student at Balliol, whom Raphael had tried remorselessly to recruit, Dennis was one of his dearest friends, dying in his early fifties. Raphael had helped carry his coffin.

Highgate held no personal associations for me, but it seemed appropriate as a civic space open to all comers (all who could pay, that is: in 1996 the grave, or rather the right of burial for seventy years in the grave space numbered 52084, cost £2,500). I liked the unconventional memorials and the mix of statuary: writers with their open books, scientists with obelisks, the unorthodox figures among the more usual angels. Highgate's community of the dead was cosmopolitan and multi-faith or of no faith at all. Plots, though, could not be booked in advance; one must take what was offered.

So many people loved Raphael I could see no way of making an invidious choice between family and friends for a private service in Highgate's chapel. We had no children to patrol that boundary either. Raphael had always loved a crowd and somehow, without any public announcement in the press, more than three hundred people turned up, and the funeral took on its own organic form. The coffin left not from Elder Street but from the house of our friends Stuart and Catherine Hall, who lived nearer to the cemetery, and under whose care I could shelter. It also put me in a more public role. The pall-bearers – my brother Chris, Gareth Stedman Jones, Robin Blackburn and Tariq Ali – manfully carried the coffin uphill with the long procession of mourners trailing behind as if at a village funeral. Up it went, past the enormous Stalinist gargoyle erected by the British Communist Party in 1956 on Karl Marx's grave. Raphael loathed that monument and reckoned Marx, who had chosen to be buried without ostentation in a domestic plot with his wife, Jenny, would be equally appalled. Up and on the procession went, to the top of the cemetery opposite Waterlow Park. I'm not sure whose idea it was to book a Scottish piper or why, though it added to the sense of occasion and Raphael would have loved the serendipity.

In the spirit of a History Workshop, no one was turned away. My family and Raphael's stood with the students, fellow historians, old comrades and neighbours at the graveside while Raphael's friends read poems or tributes. No singing, though – what songs might we have had in common? The 'service' was later published in the journal which Raphael had founded, much like the obituaries of ministers to be found in Dissenting magazines, but there was little Christianity. John Walsh, historian of primitive Methodism, chose an extract from one of John Donne's *Meditations*, 'All mankind is of one author, and is one volume', and I requested the beautiful lines from the Book of Common Prayer, with the image of death as at once violent, senseless and utterly natural – how

a life 'cometh up, and is cut down, like a flower'. Since I had
no family religion I could not be offended by flouting trad-
itions. I wore a new green hat with a wide brim and felt elated
and frivolous, smiling, greeting, embracing scores of people.
Someone had set up a microphone for speakers and, though
no one had warned me, a photographer from the *Guardian*
newspaper appeared, adding to a sense of theatre. I was almost
entirely outside my own body as I threw the first handful of
soil on top of the coffin, a common-enough sensation at
funerals, I'm sure.

That evening alone at home, I knew none of it had happened. The illness, the death, the funeral were all a dream or
a hoax, and I waited to hear Raphael's key in the door, and
him calling 'Honey?', and the thud of his bag in the hall. 'He
wasn't buried today,' I wrote in my diary, 'what is real is what
goes on inside.'

★

I never felt 'Raphael' was there – up at Highgate, in the
grave – yet the thought of his body decomposing twisted my
heart; his 'poor bones', as I saw them, 'on the cold hillside'
echoing my own feelings of abandonment. His physical presence had been wrenched from me and I hung on to it in any
way I could. I wore his jumper and I slept in his bed; I did
what the bereaved do. 'He's gone,' I said to Sally, on his sixty-
second birthday on Boxing Day, a day when I delighted to
give him a second round of presents. But I had no idea of
where he was. Shock is a kind of incredulity and despite all I
had done to make his death real to me, these feelings of disbelief returned over the weeks and months.

Perhaps that is why I wrote so much. Like the Ancient Mariner I rehearsed in my diary the story of his dying, absorbing it in ink. I typed up the fragments of autobiography he had recorded and the interview we did together; I filled a box file and the inevitable A3 ring binder with anecdotes and observations, physical descriptions and characteristic phrases; I made notes on what he had told me of his childhood, on our marriage, on his work, on what we called his 'Communist unconscious'. I couldn't stop writing and my hands went furiously on and on like the red shoes in Hans Christian Andersen's fable, cut off from the rest of my being. I was restless and, at times, euphoric. I accumulated thousands of words.

Most of it was biographical – preserving his 'bios', his life. It was also a way of staying close to him. Scribbling random notes on the back of used paper, I was impersonating him. Behaving like the lost person, employing their gestures, finding that you use, quite involuntarily, their turns of phrase, is a common response to loss. It's a version of the searching which confirms the absence but also incorporates the presence of the dead, making tangible and visible again what perishes first of all – the body of the beloved. In the months to come I understood better the myth of Mausolus, whose widow eats his ashes. What easier way to take in a death and to digest its consequences (what therapists call 'internalizing')? For me, words were necessary to this introjection; I was looking for ways to feed on my loss.

Perhaps too it was a last-ditch attempt at playing God, a compensation for the helplessness I'd felt watching Raphael die. I hadn't been able to stop that happening but now I felt that I, and I alone, had the key to his life. I was preparing the materials for a vast biography: 'Chapters in the Life of Raphael Samuel'. At the same time I imagined producing a succinct, authoritative piece which would allow me to have the last word. I see now that writing also kept the grief at bay (though I collapsed periodically, leaning against the house walls for support or lying doubled up on the bathroom floor); that words were insulation and ballast, staving off the sense of weightlessness, the untethering which makes the bereaved kindred to the mad.

Of course I had to abandon the 'article' – editing, cutting or finishing anything about Raphael's life was psychologically impossible. As well as being grateful, I was taken aback by how swiftly Raphael's closest male friends could write about him, how readily they occupied the public space. Perhaps mistakenly, I linked their capacity to find that authority with a different relation to grief, one in which anger was more allowable (and triumphal feelings too). Getting something out of your system – and that includes writing about it – requires aggression; writing alienates. I found myself wondering whether, compared with their male peers, women have always written less about the death of people they loved. So many of the women who wrote to me tried to imagine how I felt; the men wrote of their own grief. Both could help. Or not.

Grief is always incommensurate and overwhelming. To others it so often seems melodramatic. Could I have protected myself from the deluge? I'm old enough now to have caught up with other widows, or, rather, for them to have caught up with me. I have seen them stagger and go under as I did, although they have been bereaved in the fullness of time. I wasn't saved by being younger, though according to the propitiatory homilies offered by acquaintances, being married 'only ten years' ought to make it easier; nor was it worse, as far as I can tell. I did not feel I had my life ahead of me, no matter how many well-meaning souls told me I was 'still young'. I felt far older than they. What was 'my life'? A curtain had fallen across it. Without Raphael, what lay ahead was so dark, so impenetrable, there was no passage or passing of time, no sequence – no way through the woods, yet.

If we knew, as all the old songs always say, if we knew, if we could *bear* to know (but of course we do know and we risk it every time), how terrible it is to lose someone, we would never love. The human bargain. Love in exchange for death.

★

Mourning, I wrote in my diary, felt 'like a gaping wound in my stomach which might start to bleed at any moment'. I wished I had an armband so that strangers in shops would be gentle with me and acquaintances might not ask, 'How are you?' At other times I loved the anonymity of London, its 'grey immensity', Henry James's phrase, whose fiction I was rereading, wrapping myself up in his long, finely discriminating sentences. Within a few weeks a memorial was being planned. I sat at meetings and could only feel Raphael being taken away from me piece by piece as speakers were suggested to represent different parts of his life. How to share mourning when, as our friend Barbara said to me, 'only you know what you have lost'? Yes, and the timescale of mourning, which was always out of kilter with that of others: six months, a year, two or three years on and they would say, 'Is it really that long?', disbelieving. For them time has gone precipitately fast; their grief has been a thread woven through their lives but not the whole tapestry.

I made my own private and self-conscious ragbag of ceremonies. I made montages of photographs of us together and one of Raphael in his off-duty moments, in a pinny cooking dinner, walking the Cornish cliffs or in his swimming trunks. I fashioned an album of our love letters. I could not take his shirts to the charity shop until I had listed them – 'soft brown/ green dogstooth flannel, Made in Rumania' – one of many inventories, a basic, if manic, form of preservation. After a month or so I moved back upstairs to our double mattress in the attic and left his photograph downstairs. Forty-nine days I knew from the *Tibetan Book of the Dead* to be when the soul ceases to be in transition: I lit a fire and burnt Raphael's sumptuous dressing gown, the 'Oblomov' robe, upstairs in the open grate. Did I believe in these rituals? That was beside the point. They comforted me and they passed the time, and that was enough.

Six hundred people at London's Conway Hall for a memorial in late April: it was packed to the rafters and I was bathed in affection. None of this made me less territorial, even though I knew it was pointless to try to monopolize the dead. When someone commented, 'There are so many widows here today,' I wanted to shout, 'NO, I AM THE ONLY ONE!' I felt again the pressure to be generous, a sort of *noblesse oblige* to come second, and this still seems to me to be right. I was not the most important person that day. Raphael was.

Raphael never fitted the image of the great public man. Nearly all the obituarists in the press, all male, made personal comments on his appearance, his voice and his home, usually affectionately; *The Times* averred that women always wanted to look after him. Even when the writers warned me that editors had 'hacked to pieces' their copy, any mistake, however tiny, felt like a desecration, as if they were vultures hovering above the body which was already to them a memory and to me was still living. They got facts wrong – his date of birth, his age at death – or dreamt up 'factoids', those strange hybrids, established by a vertiginous series of Chinese whispers or journalistic sleight of hand. The *Guardian* columnist, keen to assume that Raphael chose to be buried near Marx, transformed the public nature of the funeral into the 'death of an era' and of an older socialism. Oedipal knives were occasionally out now that Raphael could no longer argue back. Fury, glee and psychic debris floated across the ether towards me, mixing with the flow of love and admiration.

I was crazed by the urge to correct and inform until I realized this could become a lifetime's work. 'You will have to give up the right of reply,' Cora wisely cautioned me. Better to accept that everything written about Raphael had its fantasies, its unconscious: 'The Pied Piper of History Workshop', one obituarist dubbed him, fondly scaling down to size the solemnities of his soubriquet as 'the People's Historian' but also inadvertently infantilizing Raphael's comrades. A friend in the US wrote to say she had heard that Raphael had 'slipped away surrounded by friends'. I knew it to be untrue. We were alone, he and I, and he had fought for his last breath. But should I disenchant her? I too had interpreted Raphael's dying – the 'Bolshevik' death, the 'good' death. I had written letters that made a narrative, to his doctors, to my parents and to many of his closest friends. Symbolically at least, in a sense that mattered, he *had* died surrounded by friends.

'Nothing is lost,' wrote another historian, commenting rightly on how memory survives. I was enraged. Nothing is lost! The *man* himself was gone. The freshly bereaved does not want memory but actuality; not the simpering monument or the brightly lit legacy but the old, used, soiled body, the cage and shell – the trashy flesh, so disdained and relegated, the person in their entirety. That dear material, lost for ever.

★

Raphael had failed miserably to acquire what Wemmick, Dickens's upwardly mobile clerk in *Great Expectations*, calls 'portable property'. Most of the personal items on his desk – a Victorian paperweight, a little whiskey glass shaped like a thistle – were gifts from me. There were no family heirlooms. He never wore a watch until my parents gave him one; had no rings other than his wedding ring; no expensive clothes, apart from the Italian leather jacket bought as a hostage to fortune on our last holiday in Bellagio, which I gave to a young relative. A few relics were special to me: the tiny battered frying pan, encrusted and blackened, with a burnt Bakelite handle, in which he cooked bacon at 6 a.m. before setting off for Ruskin (the aroma would drift up to the attic, whispering me awake); a packet of Old Holborn tobacco that had somehow survived an earlier cull, the shreds friable and wispy; and the perfectly circular breadboard which Raphael produced in woodwork lessons at school, proud evidence of an unlikely and never repeated skill.

But the house – what was I to do with that? At first it was a baleful reminder, day in and day out, of his absent presence.

Every room had decades of his files and was crammed with his books. My own contribution to our library, the difference I had made, seemed suddenly very meagre; with Raphael gone, it was me who dwindled. I couldn't bear, I told Cora, 'just being a chapter in Raphael's life'. She answered gently but boldly, 'Perhaps you can't bear Raphael becoming a chapter in yours.' Mostly I felt unentitled. Unentitled to the house, which was now mine; to a widow's pension from the teachers' union, a small monthly amount of £250, and the unexpected and to me vast lump sum of £34,000, a year of Raphael's salary, which went with it. I could use the money towards cataloguing the archive and I could take time off from work for a while, but the house weighed on me as if it were not my home. Why was I living in Spitalfields? My connection, despite ten years, felt flimsy. I was not, like Raphael, a Londoner with antecedents in the East End or a historian drawn to the area; or a conservationist intent on restoring eighteenth-century houses. The small circle of neighbours on Elder Street knew me as Raphael's wife, and my relationship to him stood in the foreground and overshadowed us all. I felt, as widows and widowers do, like only half a person.

A museum was the answer, I thought. I'd long had the idea of making the house a research institute for studying East London (when I told Raphael, he was very moved by the idea but commented, 'I think I'd rather be around for it'). Now I would keep it as a museum and an archive where scholars could come to use Raphael's papers. I wrote excitedly to my parents announcing my plans and making it clear that I would not gain financially from Raphael's death. At night I lay awake in a hectic state, feverishly working out the practicalities of going on living in a museum that could be open once or twice a week. There was a precedent of sorts. Our Californian neighbour, Dennis Severs, around the corner in Folgate Street, gave tours of his home as a 'Spitalfields experience' on certain nights. His fine historical imagination, not overburdened with a sense of accuracy, had created an atmosphere of the past by insisting on silence from visitors as street cries and the sounds of horses' hooves on cobbles were played through hidden speakers; the life of an imagined family was conjured by the remains of a meal on the table. The past was for him like the *Marie Celeste*.

Mine would not be a museum of Spitalfields, though it might hold exhibitions now and then, but a place to generate work. The museum dedicated to Raphael would continue our life together. I did not see how Gothic this fantasy was, myself as a pale concierge, spookily inviting visitors in, and conducting them to their places as the cobwebs gathered and the house, like Miss Havisham's wedding feast, grew more and more decayed, the clocks for ever stopped at two in the morning and the date always fixed at 9 December 1996.

It did not last, this *idée fixe*, but it was not a matter of time. In those early months, when every day is unmitigated, eventless, hourless, amorphous, measurement falls away. Suffice it to say that the museum, or the mausoleum, was a refusal and a longing. I wanted my heart to break. I listened to it, beating at night remorselessly – 'I am, I am' – and willed it silent. It just went on. And on.

*

As a schoolboy, Raphael was against ghosts, though he reckoned, somewhat ruefully, that historians ought really to credit them since every life leaves traces. I, on the other hand, was brought up to believe in them, or at least to keep an open mind. A country aunt told us in a matter-of-fact way of a poltergeist in their remote cottage who moved the chairs and laid the table at night. In the huge, modern department store where my mother worked, a colleague could 'smell death', intuiting its imminence or presence when approached by a customer, and at school, a fellow pupil with second sight was a great asset at seances. Closer to home, one of my mother's sisters and her Irish husband became fanatical spiritualists. So successful were they at calling up the dead that my cousin Michael was driven, my mother said, to leave home, fed up with the temperature in the living room suddenly dropping to freezing in the middle of summer.

Illness, dying and death were frequent topics among the grown-ups, and while we had no family graves, our local public cemetery was a solemn place, where children did not dare to venture. We antidoted our fear of ghosts by playing in St Mary's churchyard nearby among the old stones, scaring each other gleefully with the gruesome 'Hearse Song', and wailing its banshee chorus:

> The worms go in, the worms go out,
> They go in thin, they come out stout,
> Your brains come tumbling down your snout,
> OO-ooh! AA-aah! A hundred years from now.

One night in the attic bedroom I heard rats in the linen basket. It was 2 a.m., the hour that Raphael had died. At other times in the dark I was sure a stranger was coming up to the bedroom and I lay unable to breathe. I was skinless, unbounded. Super alert to every sound. The horror of death was inside me and projected on to the world. I was reminded of the story 'The Monkey's Paw', which terrified me as a child. A mother wishes for her son's return after he dies in an accident and her wish is granted. Then the realization dawns that he will come back in his shroud from the grave as he was, rotting and broken. Did the longing for the dead to play their part in our lives again mask a more taboo, unspoken need for the dead to stay dead? In this strange liminal time, on the boundary between life and death, and at the witching hour, a door had been opened, and I stood on its threshold.

And then the door *was* broken down. I heard the sound of wood splitting and wandered downstairs one evening, only to stand transfixed as the front door began to leave its hinges, the frame to splinter and the wood to gash. We lived, as many people did then, with a single Yale lock. But the old wood saved me. Heavy eighteenth-century oak, waxing and waning with the weather, it stuck fast and whoever – or whatever – was on the other side gave up and went away. I thought of the strongest, biggest man I knew living locally, Bill Schwarz, a History Workshop editor, and rang him. Bill came and stayed the night. Next morning a locksmith fitted a slender metal reinforcement around the door frame, known in the trade as a 'London strip'. He had been installing quite a few in Spitalfields. As conservation made the houses pricier and the area was more on the radar of the City, petty economic crime was on the rise. Not a revenant from the other world then, but more likely a lost soul in this.

If fear came in the night, desire began to lacerate my days. My body was a mess. I had cramping pains in my abdomen which turned out not to be cancer as I half hoped but acute colitis, my old complaint, bringing sweats and vomiting.

During Raphael's illness I had been eating for two and was ten stone six (66kg), two stone overweight. And now I was beset by a series of hopeless, girlish infatuations. Crushes. Obsessive thoughts, sexual fantasies, to the point, almost, of stalking. All my objects were unsuitable, or, rather, unavailable, and therefore *suitable* for my proliferating desires. I needed them to be unrequited, and my good angel (I think of this as a personification of Raphael's love) protected me from abuse. Once or twice a ghoul was attracted to my misery. Mostly I unconsciously found people who could do me little harm, who were firmly attached to others, or rightly wary of my advances, sensitive enough to respect my condition, or so narcissistic as to be impermeable. Few became friends, though Peter, one of my colleagues, did. Despite – or because of – his being gay, I made a pass at him. He was too well mannered to make much of it but was happy to squire me on occasion to films or the theatre, and to play the role of the pleasure principle while he went on with his own adventures.

The days passed in febrile daydreams, a reverie distracting me from everyday misery, and the repetitive, shameful small voice which kept asking, 'Will anyone ever love me again?' The crushes gave me something to look forward to, to dress up for. I grew my hair; I coloured it; I plucked my eyebrows and painted my nails. Someone told me of a new 'fitness centre' on Bishopsgate open to the general public; I joined and lost weight. I bought new clothes – tarty leather skirts, impossibly high heels – and put on perfume. I was back in adolescence but could not imagine or remember how one went to bed with anyone. In my diary I wrote about the early days of my courtship with Raphael, how we did not need drink or drugs, only talk and the wild stimulus of each other's company

before we spontaneously 'fell into each other's arms'. I wanted
to be in love but without a lover, to forget myself, to be
touched, stroked, held, kissed. To be desired but to be a
child again.

Friends, of course, dear friends, put their arms around me,
kept up the flow of solicitousness; but night after night,
morning after morning, I woke like millions of others do, to
a kind of howling non-existence. I came first for no one. No
longer the apple of anyone's eye. And on those days, which
inevitably became more frequent, when I felt some respite, I
mourned that too: I mourned the mourning, knowing that,
like the body in the grave mouldering away, it was already no
longer what it once was.

Often I spent my nights in a fugue of reproachful dreams,
looking for Raphael in crowded hospital wards, madhouses
and, worst of all, ghastly parties, knowing I had abandoned
him. I would wake up sweating and turn on all the lights.
One night I dreamt there was a wolf on the prowl deep down
in the basement kitchen, hungry and restless, while I sat up in
bed fully conscious, waiting. The dream left me troubled for
days. I had found it exciting. Out of which cubbyhole of the
unconscious, what repertoire of childhood fairy stories, did
that wolf come softly padding from his primeval forest?
Whose was the devouring appetite? I might think that I
wanted to die, but the desire to live kept coming back to
haunt me.

10   Duettino

After Raphael died, his mother and I were widows together in a close but curiously anomalous companionship. We found the asymmetry of our ages – forty-one and eighty-seven – satisfying and liberating. Minna offered me Bill's study, overlooking the garden, to write in and liked me to turn up unannounced, to come and go as I pleased. We were each other's minders. Most days she rang me with abrupt, rather pointless bulletins, and I told myself that these calls kept her going, though they were, I see now, a lifeline too for me.

She was the opposite of possessive; we could talk without constraint about Raphael and when I was with her, eating her horrible food off plastic dishes to save on washing up, I felt him very near, at once exasperated by his mother and proud of her free-spiritedness. Minna never hesitated to tell me, when I needed to hear it, how precious I had been to Raphael, and because she had loved him so much I could be consoled by her as I could not be by my own mother. Whether by temperament, generation or politics, Minna was never one for introspection, but I could say anything to her – how I felt I had let Raphael down (which widow doesn't reproach herself?); how I felt bullied by Raphael's reputation and the expectations of friends and relatives – and she would weigh it rationally and answer without flannelling. She did not try to second-guess how I felt and that was a relief too. Nor could I put myself in her shoes, though I could see how broken up she was.

I would arrive at Princes Risborough station, shaking the
London streets from my feet, and wander up the overgrown
footpath out the back of the car park, climb over a stile on to
Shootacre Lane, and follow it out of the town until it faced
the open fields on the other side of the road, with the Chilterns
in the distance. Minna might be in the garage or, more likely,
catching up on the BBC news. She and Bill had always lived
frugally, but she had her old-age pension and her music had
brought her a wealth of new friends and contacts. They had
decamped to the sticks for Bill's sake, ostensibly. Yet how
would she have dedicated herself to music if she had lived in
the vicinity of her family or made what he called her 'racket'
in a London flat? After he died in 1995 she might have lived
closer to her relatives, been safer, and made life easier for
everyone. But she never made the move.

One broiling June day I turned up, depressed and restless.
Mahler was playing full blast and in the cluttered, greasy
kitchen, clad only in a sleeveless vest and slacks, Minna was
frying a large kipper that she had just fancied. Bill gone,
Raphael dead, her beloved sister Miriam too, and so many
others. 'How do you go on?' I asked her, in a moment of my
own despair. 'I get up in the morning and I work. I don't ask
the big questions any more.' Flat-chested and slightly
whiskered, she seemed to have transcended her gender and
her age, at once both a girl and an elderly man, part Ariel,
part Prospero.

For a while contemporary music, much of it hot off the
press, became part of my life. Minna had edged me towards
her tastes over the years with birthday presents selected in
advance from a music catalogue. She hated having to cast
about for gifts. Like Raphael she was nerve-racked by

surprises and usually let the cat out of the bag. She introduced me to Schnittke, Bloch, Bruch, Schoenberg's *Gurrelieder*, all on the cusp of the new musical language which had transformed her own life when she went back to composing in her seventies after a forty-year gap. I found her music thrilling but tough, even exhausting. At times its restless energy reminded me of Raphael at his most frenetic or argumentative. At the Proms I had kept quiet about enjoying John Tavener's mesmeric *The Protecting Veil*, a piece reflecting his Russian Orthodox faith, which was on the programme with Minna's symphony. She thought it 'wishy-washy'.

Sometimes I accompanied Minna to concerts and we went on cross-country journeys to music festivals (at Aldeburgh I hurried to keep up as she hobbled with her walking stick at full speed along the seafront, galvanized by excitement). The music scene was sociable and I found composers an easy bunch to hang out with; perfectly friendly, full of their own work, they asked little of me. I admired the way that Minna resisted chronology and went on composing. She took applause in her stride, proud of her achievements, refusing to be coy. Her body, though, was catching up with her and she could work only for an hour or so most days. She did not expect to live to finish her latest composition, a second string quintet. Her determination gave me heart, though there was ruthlessness in it too. Bill had broken out one day, she told me, with the almost unforgivable accusation 'Dammit, woman, your music is more important than I am!' Without thinking Minna had replied, 'It's more important than *I am*!'

Now that all her music was being played and recorded she was something of a celebrity. Given her unusual 'career', she was also treated by the media as a Geriatric Phenomenon, invited on to chat shows and featuring in books on how to make the most of old age; BBC Two devoted a television documentary to her entitled *A Life in Reverse*, a phrase she used about her rejuvenation through music. Journalists frequently remarked on the contrast between the little old lady in her eighties who might be expected to be 'watching soaps and knitting socks' and the passionate music which issued from her. Her childhood in London's impoverished East End, her winning a place at the Royal Academy but needing to give up music after a couple of years in order to help her mother and sisters in the shop: the highlights of her story conjured a Romantic tale of artistic struggle with the return to music as its inevitable finale. Her years in the British Communist Party were rarely mentioned; perhaps they were seen as an embarrassment.

Yet I knew from Minna that in the 1930s and 1940s she had been utterly preoccupied by political activity. She had never, she said, felt nostalgic for music, not even owning a wireless. Joining the Party was not a digression. It had emancipated her. It liberated her from a stifling life as a respectable Jewish housewife (she always thought 'entertaining' a waste of time) and freed her from a religion she no longer believed in. The Party gave her a new social life where she could learn to argue and find confidence in herself; and it offered her a cause to believe in, fighting fascism, in a movement, as she saw it, for the betterment of others. Although she left the Party in 1957 after the revelations about Stalin's Terror and the invasion of Hungary by Soviet troops, Minna stayed a left-winger all her life. I was often startled by her comments on what she called 'the anarchy of capitalism' as we watched the news together.

Minna's return to music was partly happenstance. Privately tutoring a few schoolchildren in piano during her retirement, she met a young composer, Justin Connolly, who came to examine one of her pupils. He took an interest in Minna's student work and urged her to go back to writing. Without Raphael's gift of composition lessons with Connolly, she could not have afforded it and she might have stayed, as she put it, in an autumnal mood.

★

I was thinking of myself, of course, as I listened to Minna's memories and pieced her life together. I too was looking for inspiration from Minna's old age, even though I no longer believed that an individual could simply forge their life by sheer force of will. What kind of future would *I* have and how would *I* grow old? I was 'only' in my mid forties, as everyone kept reminding me, but I felt prematurely aged, out of sync with my generation and also with my parents', having seen my husband die. I might be acting like an adolescent – getting drunk, having crushes – but my body told a different story as it headed into menopause. Sometimes I longed for a baby, now that it was almost certainly too late, and I knew that I was longing for a future. I did not know what age I was. I had no peers and often felt adrift, not liberated. I wasn't 'single'. I was a widow and a different kind of spare part.

What lay in store? Was there an art to ageing? My mother and father had just retired and moved into sheltered housing, where, at sixty-four and seventy, they were among the youngest of the residents. Their small block of flats dismayed me;

they had joined the 'old people'. The entrance smelt of cabbage and air freshener; a deadened silence hung in the carpeted corridors, enlivened by occasional bursts of overly loud televisions. My father seemed depressed by the move. He missed pottering about in the old house and felt cooped up in the one-bed flat, despite the proximity of the seafront and their daily walks. On the ground floor, the patch of grass outside their French windows looked straight on to the car park. Like many men after a long working life, he also missed the camaraderie of his workmates and having a job to do. Neither of my parents could talk much about Raphael; they were facing forward. 'Will that be *it* then?' Dad asked belligerently, when I mentioned footnoting *Island Stories*, as if Raphael was demanding this of me. It was as though I had to abandon Raphael entirely to have a life of my own. And perhaps my father was angry that he had failed to protect his daughter from this ultimate desertion.

Self-centred as all mourners are, I made few allowances. I saw stagnation where they saw potential release; I saw a narrowing down of their lives where they saw the opportunity to expand. My father went to work at thirteen, destined to be a bricklayer, though the war put paid to his apprenticeship. A series of strenuous jobs working six days a week for most of his life had scarred his health and he was tired. My mother, in a shop at fourteen, pregnant at sixteen, bringing up three children, dreamt of that Shangri-La of peace and quiet that was never possible in the noisy terraced streets of Fratton. Much that I took for granted and no longer saw as luxuries – holidays, wine, occasional lie-ins and, above all, being in charge of my time – would come to them only in retirement; that, and a bit of money from downsizing, which they had never had before. As was the custom in their upbringing, they did not want to depend on their children in old age. They were also reassured that, 'whoever goes first', the one left alone would be able to cope.

In time their sociability found its natural level. My father became the go-to handyman for helpless widows in their nineties and an ad hoc groundsman, planting and watering the communal flower beds. My mother cast an actuarial eye over the block's joint finances and saw to the costing of new carpets or the window cleaning. Both were stalwarts of meetings, hailed wherever they went, and sitting in their shorts on their stripy deckchairs, sunbathing on their square of lawn, they exchanged the time of day with passers-by. Fratton, in other words, came to Southsea. My mother relished the company of the older generation, her mother's age group, especially the 'ladies' there, retired teachers, naval officers' wives, whose long lives fascinated her. Dad found solace in solitary Sunday-morning cycle rides along the prom. In its way their rejuvenation was as impressive as Minna's. But how would I find another lease of life?

As the twentieth century ebbed to its close I decided to rent a place out of London for a while, to get some distance from Spitalfields. I took a small terraced house on Osney Island, a sequestered district surrounded by the Thames in Oxford. I lived alone and left Elder Street in the care of a lodger, popping back at weekends and for a therapy session on Monday afternoons. In a reprise of my trips to Princes Risborough, I'd arrive at Oxford station late in the evening and walk up the Botley Road, my feet echoing over the metal footbridge to West Street. In the darkness the rush of a mill race greeted me, then the rustle of trees, the smell of mud, and I sensed the bulky shape of St Frideswide's church hunkered down behind a spur of the river.

I wanted a distance from Minna too, though that was harder to admit. We still talked regularly and she was mentally very vigorous but her health was faltering. In Stoke Mandeville hospital she was a great hit with the nurses, only wishing that they wouldn't always switch the piped radio to 'light' music. The family stepped in, visiting regularly, and making it possible for Minna to be looked after at home, but I kept away. I could not bear to see her in a weakened state looking so much like Raphael. I felt I had 'supped full of horrors'. No one chided me, though I felt I was failing her. There was to be no Jewish burial, since Minna requested a secular ceremony and cremation like Bill's. Bill's ashes were stowed away under a tree in their garden but the house would have to be sold. We put Minna's at the foot of Raphael's grave.

January, February, March, and into the spring of the new century (the symbolism appealed to me) I took long walks in Oxford along a riverbank edged with purple loosestrife, past the Binsey poplars, pausing now and then to watch the cows chew. Like them I was a ruminant. Gradually I went back to the book about Virginia Woolf's cook, Nellie Boxall. That relationship looked less one-sided now, despite the differences of power and privilege. I no longer saw dependence on others as something simply to be feared but as a central part of any life, of any human society. I shuffled old notes around and sat in the early sunshine in my rented garden.

But how to tell a life? As it happened, Minna's obituary was the first I ever wrote. I knew that her late flourishing owed as much to chance as to self-direction, and that a life was always shaped by others in the crucible of history. And I was struck by how obituary, biography's twin, shares that sleight of hand which creates the sense of an ending. Retrospectively it gives value to a life, as we all need to do, for those who die. But would Minna's life not have been equally valuable if she had never returned to music?

Minna had often talked of living her life 'in reverse', but I thought her old age had become a gathering, an incorporation of her former selves, and a making anew. In 1929, when, as shy Minnie Nirenstein, she left off composition, Debussy was the most avant-garde composer in her pantheon. His lyrical piano chords ripple through her student pieces, as do the dissonances, breaking expectation, heralding another tonal world for which another musical language would be needed. Sixty years later, Minna Keal's *Cantillation* was far more uncompromisingly modernist in its idiom, but the piece, like its title, harked back to her childhood, to the chants of the cantor in the synagogue, to her uncle Leibel's playing of the violin and to Feigel, her mother, singing Hebrew folk songs. 'I'm a hybrid,' Minna liked to say of herself. That was what I wanted. Not a plot or a progress but a being in the present, whatever it brought, fully alive.

Minna always assumed that I would move from Elder Street, and when she died she smoothed my way into the future. She left her house to me and to Bill's son, Hugh, which gave me a tidy sum. So thanks to her and to Raphael, two ex-Communists, I had a mortgage-free home and modest means. For the third or fourth time in my life, heading towards fifty, I decided to devote more time to writing, but in the years to come I often found my way back to teaching, running out, yet again, of steady funds, but also needing to be kept on my

mettle, and wanting to go on learning. Of course, chance, the
wild card, often intervened. Like many women, I suppose I
have been a late starter, but at what? The stopping and stalling,
the turning aside, is also a way of life.

A portrait of Minna by her friend Ray Waterman.

11 Acts of Recovery

In April 1997, when I spoke at Raphael's memorial, I took with me his home-made cookbook as a visual aid for the audience. Another of his unwieldy A3 lever-arch files, its recipes were written on loose sheets, napkins and old menus, pasted in from newspapers or scribbled down in a phone call. Over the years it had become a mini history of food and a directory of all those lovers, family members, colleagues and passing comrades who had supplied him with ideas for meals. I stood on the stage of the Conway Hall in London and read out names and dishes at random amid much laughter (although I did not divulge the source of the legendary cheesecake whose ingredients Raphael kept a closely guarded secret from the History Workshop collective). The file was testimony to Raphael's endless curiosity, his appetite for knowledge and to his being fed by others. It also was a way of levelling: 'Miriam's latkes' were no more or less exotic than 'Barbara's English breakfast'.

From Raphael I learnt that everything was a potential source, everything was in a state of becoming history. After he died I turned up a document wallet marked 'Alison and Raphael'. Inside were all our letters and lovers' tokens, every birthday and valentine, which for Raphael were a new habit – 'your card culture', he dubbed it – and every domestic reminder we left each other as we went off to work. These scraps give glimpses of our life together: what we ate, who

made supper; who did the shopping and where. 'Honey, I
have gone to bed,' my notes often begin, and his, 'Sweetheart,
please wake me', me craving sleep and he paring it to a minimum. I can see that even the well-being of Morgan, 'comrade
cat' – whether he had been fed or not, for instance – could
express our moods, our language of mutual care and demand.
As revealing as the lengthy courtship letters we wrote each
other, these throwaway lines are less of a performance.

Raphael's attachment to the past extended far beyond
preserving the written record, to a compassion for the weathered and worn which bore the marks of time. The scratch on
an old LP brought back a drunken evening; the holes in a
shirt pocket from a fag-end not quite extinguished, or the
stains where a pen had leaked, were like the patina of age on
a building, signs of past human culture. The elegiac, though,
can easily become nostalgic. Loss, in other words, has to be
worked on. The file of our domestic notes, like the cookbook,
was material for future use. As a historian, Raphael was closer
to the rag-and-bone man of my childhood, more of a recycler
than an antiquarian or conservationist.

Raphael was happy for his life to be historicized: he preferred to be seen as representative. Yet as I began sorting
through his papers to make an archive, I observed myself creating levels of intimacy, donating some personal letters and
keeping others back. I wanted an inner sanctum where others
could not reach; I resisted and resented the way history lays
its hand on even the most private areas of our lives, revealing
them to be of their time. As a species of public widow, I
thought I was in a special position, particularly exposed, particularly effaced. Now I believe that what I felt was only an
exacerbation of that tug of war which pulls everyone apart

when a beloved person dies and whose different claims are never resolved: when to hold on, when to share and when to relinquish.

★

Widows, widowers, 'the keepers of the flame' usually get a bad press. A spider at the centre of the web, 'the estate' controls and manipulates access, selecting materials for viewing or vetoing them, squabbling with scholars and biographers, guarding the body of work as if it were the body of the deceased. I too censored. In those first years, when I was sifting through papers, any evidence of Raphael's vulnerability felt sacrosanct: the poems full of self-loathing, written in the early 1960s on the edge of breakdown; a handful of letters written to his mother and father, full of frantic guilt towards the family and pleading to be left alone to work; the last notes Raphael made, all but illegible as his hand grew weaker. I hung on to his school reports, a few postcards written as a child and the books on which he had scrawled his name or which were part of his growing up. 'To Raphael, on your 17th birthday,' Minna had written on the flyleaf of Lewis Grassic Gibbon's *A Scots Quair*, as he was just off to Oxford, 'with love and best wishes for a year as exciting and successful as 1951 has been, from Mummy'. Each banal sentiment was a poignant fragment of a life, not to be carelessly fingered in a second-hand shop or pored over ('pawed' over) by strangers. Perhaps I wanted to go on mothering him. Even though I knew that Raphael – Ralph, Raph – had reinvented himself many times, I treated his childhood as the key to his personality, the child as father to the man. I imagined writing a memoir of his childhood, having deep insights which no one else could claim, as if I could not only regenerate his life but somehow be its origin. Such fantasies are surely at the heart of all biography whenever a biographer writes 'must have' of their subjects with all the confidence of God, the Author.

When I first gave any of his books away or packed up papers it was as if I were disturbing his physical remains. The house was so identified with him still. '19 Elder Street is a national institution,' said one friend, shortly after Raphael died, laying it on with a trowel. Another asked to 'see round the house'; another to 'say goodbye to it'. Raphael died *in medias res*, surrounded by work and leaving the essays for a second volume of *Theatres of Memory*, planned as *Island Stories*, in various states of completion. His study, next to the front door, felt full of his absence. Yet by the first anniversary of his death, working on endnotes for the volume, I had cleared and redecorated it. Rather than visit Raphael's grave, I had a party to mark the newly painted sitting room replete with couch and a fitted carpet.

It was the start of a long haul. Each cupboard on every floor was stacked with manila folders arranged thematically and tatty scripts scorched from being against hot water pipes, stained and blotted with coffee-cup circles and ash, their edges often serrated by mice. Lever-arch files flanked the staircases and landings, stood in rows on the filing cabinets and behind curtains in every room. The baize surfaces were heaped up and threatened to overflow; a large knocked-about mahogany box, stuffed with postcards and letters, obstructed the hall; the Wellington cabinet in Raphael's study was equally crammed. I had never looked into the bashed, banded trunk in my study, which might have been Raphael's student luggage, but had covered it with a rug and cushions. Dismayed, I found layers of ageing correspondence inside. Smaller card boxes lurked everywhere, even under the kitchen stairs right at the back, on top of our irascible tumble dryer, where lined file cards with references to London's workers – 'the cat's meat man' and 'the night-soil collector' – found their way into the laundry. A cobwebby pile of pamphlets and 'off-prints' from articles was squeezed high up next to the gas and electricity meters above our front door; grubby envelopes full of newspaper clippings were secreted in odd corners (at one stage Raphael employed an agency to send him every use in the press of the word 'puritan' for weeks on end). And there were thousands of books, many with Rizla cigarette papers lodged inside as book marks. Only after Raphael's death did I get to know every nook and cranny of the house I had lived in for ten years.

In his will, Raphael appointed three executors, me and his dear friends Sally Alexander and Gareth Stedman Jones, both historians. He had requested that if at all possible his papers be taken care of and deposited in some suitable institution. Of course no one would take the existing mountain of material. So we sat down to begin winnowing. Sally was fascinated by every page and reluctant to part with anything; Gareth took a brisk view of keeping drafts: 'Raphael wasn't Proust.' I veered between wanting to preserve every sheet and wishing the whole lot would go up in smoke – and me with it – overtaken by a spontaneous combustion like that which destroys old Krook and his rag-and-bottle shop in Dickens's *Bleak House*.

The chest into which a notary or a parish clerk once put documents and records was an early form of archive. It was also a model for thinking about memory as a repository, a holding environment, from which the past could be retrieved. Memory is associated with the work of retention, with hanging on to things, and yet no matter how extensive, an archive cannot represent a life, not even a working life. It could not be a museum of Raphael. No objects or bric-à-brac; no books even, though his library told its own story of his life. Friends took volumes as keepsakes and some were sold to help finance the sorting. Three thousand or so books were donated to the University of East London to enhance historical studies there. First they needed cleaning. Undaunted, my ever-loyal friend Fran stood in the backyard with me, enveloped in filthy clouds of dust, as we clapped pages together and brushed down spines. *History Workshop Journal*'s designer, Bernard Canavan, created a bookplate and I stolidly pasted one into each volume before it went out into the world.

Thankfully, the Bishopsgate Institute, where Raphael had his last office, was willing to take the papers, though there was as yet no trained archivist, only a beleaguered librarian and her assistants, and the storage conditions, especially in the basement, would need overhauling. But in other ways it was an ideal home for his work. With its Arts and Crafts façade, its crenellated towers like a miniature fairy castle, the Bishopsgate was built in 1895 opposite Liverpool Street station as a public space, offering a public borrowing library and a reference library, a hall and meeting rooms open to everyone who lived and worked in the City of London. Running courses for adults, putting on lunchtime concerts, exhibitions and lectures, it has little of that rarefied atmosphere which makes most places with archive collections remote and off-putting. Raphael had always wanted to demystify the profession and to encourage his students to see historical research as a shared enterprise. Tucking his work away in a university research centre, accessible only to a few, would have been unfortunate, to say the least. At the Bishopsgate his papers would be available to anyone who wanted to look at them, to pick up the train of his thought where he had left off and to use his insights for their own projects. They were also of a piece with the materials about London, labour and radical history which the Bishopsgate collections already held.

Any archive is a selection; there are gaps and silences. Much lands in the bin which should not; some censorship is deliberate but survivals are often arbitrary. Almost calamitously, at Ruskin College the contents of Raphael's study were emptied at random into bin liners and rescued only at the eleventh hour by Peter Claus, one of Raphael's ex-students in history. Utterly disordered, they ranged from cuttings Raphael had clipped from the *Daily Herald* as a schoolboy on the dropping of the first atom bomb, to flyers, notes and minutes from the early days of History Workshop and other political activities in the 1960s and 1970s, to his most recent correspondence. I packed up and labelled scores of boxes, which Peter and I trundled to and fro on a trolley from Elder Street up and down the main road to the Bishopsgate; more material was donated by Minna, and the dishevelled plastic rubbish bags and yet more files were transported from Ruskin. Peter tottered with his arms full up the flights of rickety stairs to store it all in a Bishopsgate annexe, a cold, dark room above a picture framer's shop. Eventually, hemmed in on all sides by the ramparts of a cardboard fortress, he began the Herculean labour of collating – not only papers and pamphlets, index cards, written and typed notes, but also photographs, audio cassettes, films and slides, annotated newspaper cuttings and

extracts from journal articles, letters and other ephemera
gathered from a variety of places over forty-odd years. Col-
lated and then inventoried, before we could even begin to
think about the cataloguing. Over four hundred boxes formed
the basis of the Raphael Samuel Collection.

As it became more official, the materials had to be stand-
ardized for reasons of preservation, if not of space. First to go
were Raphael's beloved lever-arch ring binders, their rusty
mechanisms leaving stains on the paper or warping them out
of true. I mourned their disappearance. Their much-inked
labels, endlessly repasted on the spines, told of projects reinvented or cannibalized from each other, and as their contents
disappeared into grey archive boxes to be interleaved with
acid-free papers, the physical heft of the work dissolved and
the pathways of Raphael's mind grew hazier. I wrote an elegy
of sorts to these files and to Raphael's working methods in a
biographical preface to *Island Stories*, his posthumous volume,
and was struck by how Raphael's sentences, ever capacious,
were themselves a form of hoarding, encompassing the thick
detail of the past.

The archive gave me a public role and an authority, adding
to the gravitas of the young widow. Eventually it added to my
confidence too. Perhaps it shouldn't have. Sometimes it was
easier to be Raphael's widow than his wife. People saw me
and I saw them without his dazzling presence. I got to know
a lot of his friends and made new friendships with them, once
I had the chance to talk to them alone; other times they
merged the two of us together but I felt eager to discuss him,
taking it as a tribute to the marriage. Eventually I became 'the
estate', a rubber-stamper, even a symbolic substitute. Yet as I
sat in the first-floor room upstairs in Elder Street, all but

dwarfed by teetering piles of books and mounds of paper, I wrote dolefully in my diary, 'a life doesn't amount to much'.

All archives are partial in another sense, revealing the preoccupations and predilections of those who have created them. The records of British decennial censuses, for instance, betray nineteenth-century assumptions about family life in the headings of their columns, the category 'head of household' which so infuriated women suffragists, and the insistence on a settled place. Any labelling is also a limit; the thin line between description and interpretation is one which archivists constantly tread. But no one can control an archive. Its future uses cannot be comprehensively predicted. The searcher often does not know what she or he is after and the trivial turns out to be significant. Records are read between the lines or against the grain and the archive goes on evolving through its users. I took heart from realizing that the archive was not a thing but a process, and always collaborative.

One day I found myself sitting at the Bishopsgate working with volunteers from an MA in Information Science. A student passed me a note to decipher. I had written it. Should it be kept or not? Under what heading should it be catalogued? Anthropologists might have a word for the strange magic whereby an archive user, that creature of an unknown future, finds a scrap of paper and sees it as a useful document. The domestic scrawl, the appointments diary, the bank statement, the passport photograph are suddenly transmuted into the precious and numinous, lighting up a revelatory track into the past. As a widow I experienced the opposite. Creating an official archive I learnt alchemy in reverse, turning gold back into lead; the singular and intimate made public and representative, or at least categorizable. Making the archive took many years and I had many helpers. I am still letting things go. The idea of 'closure' may be consoling and even necessary at times, but grief goes on having the power, like a valve to the heart and mind, to keep the past open.

★

Like others no longer sharing a home after divorce or bereavement, I gradually began to shape the house around how I would live in it alone, moving furniture and developing different habits. Only then, once I had adjusted to the new configuration, did I realize I did not have to live there at all. I wanted a garden and more light but a move still felt beyond me. Slowly, in my sleep, I let Raphael cross the Styx. Around the third anniversary I dreamt that he was in the US (the place, given his residual anti-American feeling, he was least likely to be). We talked on the telephone and it was good to hear from him. A connection had been made at least. Then, in the run-up to four years on, after Minna's death and with the archive well on its way, I had another dream which I took to be a psychic advance of sorts. Raphael was back. He had been away for some mysterious reason but now he had returned to Britain and I rushed round to where I knew I'd find him, slightly puzzled that he had not got in touch, but excited at the prospect of seeing him again. I dashed upstairs and knocked and there he was: wedged between columns of books and almost invisible, hunched over his desk (the setting suggested the North Gallery at the old library in the British Museum, where I used to unearth him at closing time). He was courteous and perfectly friendly but somewhat embarrassed. Clearly he was eager to get on with his work. I immediately woke up with a sad but satisfying sense that *he* had left *me* (how clever the unconscious is!): he didn't need me any more, so it was fine for me to be living my own life. This time I didn't need the Atlantic to let me off the hook.

Nearly five years on, I put the house up for sale. There were no takers. The place was too much of an oddity. Bemused businessmen hurried over in their lunch hours for viewings, puffed up and down the stairs, flabbergasted that we lived with an outside toilet, commenting in tones of mingled horror and amazement on the number of books and shelves. The months wore on and like the Lady of Shalott I saw myself immured for all time. I was rescued by our conservationist neighbour Dan Cruickshank, whose friend Basil thought he could scrape up the money to take the house on. As if still needing a kind of psychic permission, I told myself that Raphael would have approved of our avoiding estate agents altogether; I imagined him also approving the amicable bargain I struck with our friends Bill and Sarah at their Christmas party, agreeing a price on the spot for their house in nearby Stoke Newington. Five bedrooms in case I wanted lodgers and was it too late for children? Plenty of psychic room, an analyst friend suggested.

I stayed alone in Elder Street the night before the move, harbouring, as usual, my experience to myself. I had my kettle and my bed and a cup and cereal bowl for my breakfast, the last few groceries. I wanted to camp out. Most of the house contents had already been packed into the pantechnicon that had blocked the street and been taken into storage the day before. Another van would come for the last bits and pieces, and I would drive the couple of miles north up the Hackney Road to the new house. There was no cat to accompany me this time. Morgan had died a couple of years earlier at the venerable age of eighteen.

It's usual at such times, filled with a predictable sense of the momentous, to wander from room to room, remembering. A few tears would surely be in order. But next morning, when I woke up in the empty house, I felt calm and dry-eyed. The space seemed magnified. The bare, scratched panelling with the picture hooks, the battered paintwork and chipped skirting boards, the rows of empty bookshelves ready to be filled or dismantled: it was as if the house had been released from labouring under a huge burden. It felt nimble and free, no longer lumbered. It was a shell again, made by human hands, merely a hollow bounded by walls. I stood upstairs in the middle of 'the room', where we had sat on my chintzy sofa watching television to Raphael's cries of wonder, where I had dozed and dreamt my way through a hundred novels, where we first slept together on a lumpy futon mattress, long gone, and I had woken up to a breakfast of garlic and stewed tomatoes. The oak floorboards and the yellowed ceiling showed no signs of where Raphael had suffered and died. As I went downstairs, joining all those other comers and goers, I thought I could hear the house exhale.

★

An archive is a repository from which the past can be reclaimed, but for the widow it becomes a way of leaving the remembering to others. Now, after twenty-odd years, I forget what is there. I spent several days not long ago hunting for the two large box files of condolence letters I received, convinced they were somewhere about the house – for what kind

of widow parts with such materials? – until I realized where
they must be. Not exactly in the public domain. I hadn't gone
that far. But in a kind of anteroom to the archive proper,
among the boxes I had asked to be left uncatalogued and not
available to the public until their contents felt, at least to me,
less volatile.

These letters, though, are hardly explosive. They contain
no scabrous accounts of Raphael's misdemeanours, no con-
tretemps, no scurrilous details which might embarrass living
persons or involve me in diplomacy. Had I simply wanted to
put this outpouring of grief somewhere else? Now I thought
I would read them properly; I could take them in. I relished
the unconventional situation I would be in at the Bishopsgate
Institute. Unusual, surely, for a widow to sit at a desk in a
public institute and order up from its records condolence letters addressed to herself.

Where do condolence letters belong if not in limbo, half
private, half public, giving the lie to both? Raphael died at
around two in the morning on 9 December, a Monday. A few
hours later the first hand-delivered letter arrived. Word was
spreading fast in the days before email. On the 10th and 11th,
as the telephone began to chirrup incessantly and the answering machine laboured under the weight of stumbling, stricken
voices, missives of every kind landed on the mat (two posts a
day in 1996): sympathy cards with a line or two, postcards
with images that revealed so much about their senders, poems
and letters. After the first obituaries appeared in all four of the
broadsheets, I was inundated. Since Raphael and his long
association with Spitalfields was mentioned in the papers,
those who had lost touch could easily find the address in the
telephone directory. Letters came for 'Mrs Samuel' and

began, 'We have never met but . . .', or 'I don't think I ever knew him well but I've been deeply fond of him', and even 'I never met your husband but . . .' Fifty, sixty, seventy, a hundred letters and cards by the 12th, heading towards two hundred by the day of the funeral on Wednesday the 18th. The sheer weight of response to Raphael's death bespoke the urgent need to write, to keep alive that connection a day or two longer, to put off believing him dead, to put off mourning. I barely read them at the time, and answered very few; they were more nails in Raphael's coffin.

At the Bishopsgate I sat putting the condolences into rough chronological order, numbering them and pencilling in the surnames of those who did not need to say who they were. Like the busywork teachers set unruly children, it was a harmless and soothing activity, which I hoped would help Stefan Dickers, the archivist who now looks after the Bishopsgate's collections. I read them aslant, out of the corner of my eye. I observed the repeated phrases, 'generosity of spirit', 'an inspiration', almost coolly. I noted the kinds of people who wrote, though the categories overlapped hopelessly: dear friends and colleagues; Ruskin students and ex-students; my students; my colleagues; our families, including those far-flung; editors, publishers, other writers – Grub Street, as was. Letters arrived from France, Germany, Spain, Italy, the US, Brazil and Australia, and, sent on from Manchester University, a fax from the Moscow School of Sociology, where a History Workshop hand, Teodor Shanin, was trying to teach the subject free of ideology. The keepers of galleries and museums wrote, even the Scottish National Museum, where Raphael had failed to give a lecture but the curator had so warmed to his friendly refusal. With a slight feeling of vertigo, I read a card from the Bishopsgate Institute: 'impossible to imagine this place without him'. On I went, reading snatches, remarking on the repetitions, remembering faces and writing down names. Until I could do no more. My back seized up suddenly and my eyes were swimming: those awful letters, those days of almost drowning. Here I was again, needing to come up for air.

I got through one box but why was I doing it? What, after all, do condolences amount to biographically? Never speaking ill of the dead, they can hardly be trusted; so often relying on the pro forma or cliché – 'shocked and saddened', 'my heart goes out to you', 'I wish I had known him better' – they rarely aim at originality or at being more than comfortable words. 'We are thinking of you,' they say, adding the well-meaning, vague offer 'Let us know if there is anything we can do', relieving a burden of guilt towards the bereaved. Ex-lodgers wrote, ex-lovers; librarians and East End villains. So many I had never met. 'Dear Anne,' they wrote to me, and even 'Dear Hilary'. Most condolences are conventional. They are what anthropologists call a 'phatic' exchange, the ritualistic phrases, like corner-shop courtesy about the weather, which make the wheels of our common life go round.

But nearly three hundred letters by the end of January was far from usual. A letter full of feeling from one of Her Majesty's Government Inspectors of Schools; another from the manager of the History Department of Dillons bookshop on Gower Street; and another from Mick Preston, in charge of Kall Kwik, the print shop on Broad Street, where Raphael had left piles of books and put in requests for reams of Xeroxes, recalling Raphael's friendliness and genuine appreciation of what they did for him – for nearly twenty years – 'It was not just business between us.' For many, putting pen to paper was itself a tribute to the man. I could tell instantly from the penmanship or lack of it, the lined or unlined paper, the use of ink or biro, and the ease of address, how rare an event writing letters was for the correspondent. Even the more constipated prose loosened into expressions of pain: 'I loved him'; 'I am [or 'We are'] devastated', 'desolated', 'choked'. 'We wept when we heard.' An unusual phrase broke through: 'After a session with Raphael I felt as if I had been thawed out by an electric radiator on a dank November day.' Professional historians could unbutton: Raphael 'did so much good in the world', wrote Christopher Hill, his tutor at Balliol and his mentor. Some allowed themselves to be angry, feeling cheated by his death. Many commented on our marriage. Raphael, according to one friend, had 'recommended cancer for making you fall in love with your wife all over again'. Others proclaimed their own loss and barely mentioned mine: 'I don't know how to cope with this,' lamented one poor soul.

Only now could I see that, like obituaries, the condolences were a form of life-writing. Memories gave me glimpses of his growing up: 'He was a real charmer,' wrote an aunt and uncle who 'knew him from babyhood'; a 'young know-all', a cousin wrote affectionately. An old school friend thought it typical of him to be 'having a political discussion in French at the age of fifteen during his O-level French oral'; he was 'a demon' at table tennis, wrote another, while John Handford, Raphael's history teacher at King Alfred's School, in his late seventies, recalled how daunted he had been to have to teach a boy he felt already outstripped him in knowledge (it was his first year of teaching). Despite their seldom having been in touch, he was moved to say, 'I feel as if my own son has died.'

The letters brought home to me how much a life is always a community, a social being.

So many of the memories and anecdotes about Raphael saw him as a kind of secular saint if not a holy fool. He would fall asleep, they said, in the middle of tutorials; he often conducted a tutorial on a train to London; and, my particular favourite, when a dog wandered into the lecture hall at Ruskin where Raphael was talking on nineteenth-century history, he immediately made the stolen dog trade in the East End the subject for discussion. One post brought me an obituary by his uncle Chimen Abramsky for the *Jewish Chronicle*, comparing him to the nineteenth-century Russian Narodniks, revolutionary populists and utopians; another a note from Sheridan Gilley, historian of Christianity, half joking that if Raphael had been a Catholic, he would have been in danger of instant canonization. Raphael once wrote an essay on the Irish in Britain for him 'which achieved a legendary status in typescript twenty years before it saw the light of day' (this was the work that turned Raphael into a historian, begun in breakdown in Dublin in the 1960s). They would pray for him at Mass.

The heightened moment of condolence, in the immediate aftermath of a death, allows even the most atheistical to reach for a language of the spirit, but in the humorous anecdotes and the apocryphal stories I also heard the need for models, for examples, a need which has not dwindled in a secular age among secular people who no longer turn to the life of Christ. Raphael was above all a teacher, the best kind, one who listens and who inspires, gives dignity and self-worth to the speaker, as he had to me all those years ago in the queue at the ICA. For many of its students he was the spirit of Ruskin

College: 'Whenever two former Ruskin students meet, invariably one of them will ask at some point in the conversation, "How's Raph?"' Even his physicians were moved to become his pupils: 'When I was his doctor,' wrote one, 'I faced a dilemma: I wanted to ask him questions, to learn from him and read his work, but in order to remain sufficiently detached in order to do my own job properly felt that I should not.' Listening was mentioned over and over again, as if the world is full of babble. 'He always made you feel you had something to tell him and that he urgently required it.' He had listened for two hours to an elderly lady, wrote her friend, 'who never thought she was important', probing her with questions and finding what she said so interesting, 'she thought she was the Queen of England'.

And sitting at the tables where Raphael had so often sat, I listened to all the voices, and I fell into a daze, a reverie. And in that dreaming state some miracle took place, call it a romance. The statue came back to life; the limbs were restored; Raphael was remembered. Grief turned back into love, and after the doubts and questioning in my diaries, I saw too that what we were in other people's eyes was also true: a happy marriage, a blessed companionship. 'Do you remember how you nearly didn't meet?' Minna wrote, after her hip operation, from Ward 4A in Wycombe Hospital, marvelling anew at our good fortune and gallantly making little of her own tribulations ('I've come through the op with flying colours. Loads of visitors every day so don't worry about not coming'). There too was a letter from my own mother, making good that near-disastrous occasion in Portsmouth when I first took Raphael home, an unappealing candidate for a son-in-law. Moved to a lyrical vision of her own, she conjured

'Raph striding along the seafront, hands in pockets, scarf flying and reading all the history boards'.

Outside, at a coffee stand, surrounded by bikers in leather, I blinked at the sun bouncing off the glass fronts of the multi-storey banks. Spitalfields was no longer in transition but swallowed whole into the belly of the whale. No longer an outlier of the East End but, dwarfed by skyscrapers and high-rises, it was more Wall Street than Whitechapel. It was downtown, all abuzz with people hurrying to and fro, milling around the familiar food outlets and the stalls and shops of the transformed market. It was settled. I could walk across the pedestrian precinct and look into Elder Street, and finally imagine the life I might have led if I'd stayed.

A portrait of Raphael in 1995 by our neighbour
Lucinda Douglas-Menzies.

Coda

When we buried Raphael at Highgate, the top northern corner of the cemetery was largely unmarked, mostly mud, and bleakly overlooked by the boarded-up windows of out-buildings belonging to the Whittington Hospital. The air of desolation suited me and I thought Raphael would approve of the romantic fallacy. It was of a piece with our urban walks along the Old Street canal and his sighs of sad pleasure at the dilapidated warehouses, the battered enamelled signs and derelict hoisting bays. I also liked the way that Raphael's grave faced Waterlow Park, where children were forever kicking balls and losing them in the long grass up against the fence, and mothers could be seen in the distance pushing tod-dlers or newborns up to the café, or going round and round the pond, getting a welcome breather, seemingly oblivious to the freshly dug graves close by. Perhaps they felt protected by their charges, each baby a shield.

I had chosen Portland stone for the gravestone, an old-fashioned headstone from the days when the dead were believed to be sleeping. Reminiscent of country churchyards, it was also an intellectual choice, a reference to the stonework-ers or 'marblers' of the Isle of Portland in Dorset, whom Raphael had written about in *Miners, Quarrymen and Salt-workers*, a special breed passing on their skills from father to son. My friend Frank Gray, an art historian, told me about a stonemason and engraver called John Skelton, a nephew and apprentice of Eric Gill, and together we visited his workshop near the Ditchling Beacon in Sussex, which meant a trip back to the South Downs where Raphael and I had gone blackberrying. I wanted the stone to be unmannered, so John left the back rough to show its texture; the stone has thousands of tiny fossils embedded in it. It does not weather well compared to slate or granite and in my mind's eye I imagined it crumbling back into dust.

Highgate, like other 'garden cemeteries', does not encourage terror or disgust or suicidal gloom; it is more suitable for melancholy or gentle weeping into a handkerchief. But I did not plan to loiter at the grave. In the early days I'd duck and dive to avoid the tourists down at the Marx memorial, as if there was something shameful in being an actual mourner in broad daylight. I'd turn left at Mary Ann Cross (George Eliot) and find a back way where the path was almost obliterated by brambles, trampling through the undergrowth at the top of the incline. There in a clearing I'd come upon a stone which I thought of as a warning. Put up by another widow whose husband had also died in 1996, her name and birth date were already chiselled into the slate, waiting to close her life off in brackets. She too was twenty years younger than him. I dreaded passing that spot, but eventually it invigorated me. It became a milestone.

Over the years I rarely went up to Highgate. Yet when friends told me that they could barely read the stone I felt much as my mother might have done if she hadn't swept her doorstep or polished the front brass. The grave was for others – for show. It was a historical document; it generated memory for a whole community. I had it re-engraved. I found the cemetery much sprucer when I revisited. Where pensioner volunteers used to huddle at the gate in all weathers, they now sit in the comfort of a small shop selling tickets, booklets and postcards. There are smart new watering cans, crisply gravelled paths – even toilets for visitors. And this is how it should be. 'Dark tourism' is nothing new. These grand public cemeteries were for enjoying as much as grieving, for contemplating mortality in a mood of elegiac sadness, and above all to create memories for the living. Last time I went, though, I could not bring myself to check on that stone in the clearing.

I'm supposed to be buried in Highgate: that was the original plan. Writing about graves for my last book, though, has rather put me off grave ownership. Making my own will recently, I thought I would prefer an eco-funeral: wicker basket, cremation and a woodland burial. Alternatively, since there's room, my husband John and I could make a *ménage à quatre* – a quartet at Highgate. I imagine the nonconformity would please both Raphael and his mother. At least it might give tourists pause for thought.

★

Did I believe that my suffering, though it was far from unusual, had paid some sort of debt and given me a cloak of invisibility as far as cancer was concerned? I suppose I thought that, because I had tended and nursed Raphael until he died, my own body was immune. Otherwise how can one live?

Yet there I was, with a diagnosis of my own.

Trying to count the pairs of swans afloat on the flood water of Port Meadow, I ran my fingers through my hair. Strands of it came away, so I let it waft in the breeze across the grass like dandelion down; the grey hairs went first, while the hairs on the top of my head resisted a while longer. It was confirmation that in less than a month I'd be bald. I had never seen my scalp before and now little patches of it emerged, pink and tender like uncooked sausage-skin. 'Go with the flow,' the surgeon had said, though he remained sceptical about the efficacy of the chemotherapy that was proposed after my operation. So now my hair was going and flowing. He'd also told me as I left his office, handing me over to the oncologist, that I had a much better chance of survival than those going over the top at the Somme. I did not find this cheering.

It was hard not to conflate my fate with Raphael's. Before the treatment I dreamt he was standing at the end of the bed, his face forbidding like that of an Old Testament prophet or the Angel of Death himself. It was a more ghastly version of the mourner's dilemma – wanting to separate from the beloved dead, wanting to die with them. Even a death sentence might be better, at that stage, than the awful, endless uncertainty of the diagnosis.

Four years on, as I approached my sixtieth birthday, I was given another all-clear and felt weirdly disappointed. In the hospital's underground car park my driver's door was blocked by some front-wheel-drive juggernaut, so I took my ignition key and gouged a deep, satisfying zigzag into its paintwork. Then I glanced up and saw the CCTV camera. Sick with anxiety all the way home, for the next few days I could think of little else. Why had I, guileless, harmless citizen that I usually am, why had I done it? Reason told me that such gas guzzlers are themselves a crime; in our narrow street they damage kerbstones and squat on pavements as they blithely pump out exhaust. I had often wanted to vandalize one of them, though resorted instead to leaving prissy notices of the

'Please park more courteously' variety on the windscreen. Was it revenge for the time my brand-new Skoda was 'keyed' on the first night I parked it outside, an agonized purchase which took over a year's indecision, finally abandoning my fifteen-year-old Ford? But that was months ago. Or something deeper? A delayed tit for tat (Freud would be pleased with the pun): was I getting my own back for the knife that had so casually cut into *me*?

Awake at night I was trapped in a Dostoevsky novel. I rehearsed my apology to the owner, my confession to the police, almost ill with the shame. Then one night I dreamt of my brother, Chris, and his wife, Anita. 'You're splitting up, aren't you?' I asked them in my sleep. Anita had been dead six years; her health had always been poor and after breast cancer treatment she died of fibrosis in her early fifties. Gratitude flooded me when I woke up. It was good to see her again on the cine-film of memory. I also knew now what I was guilty of. I had outlived Anita, my contemporary, and now it looked as if I would outlive Raphael. I was guilty of the worst of crimes, splitting up from him even further, heading into my sixties, not even going to die of cancer. What sort of wife was I? I wanted to be punished and my vandalism served its purpose. That guilt was easier to bear than relief.

I could go on. Dream analysis is potentially, like memoirs, interminable. There is always another history that never quite fits the one we tell ourselves. Dreams, unconscious acts and jokes: 'What would "the old man" say?' Raphael would ask me, affectionately treating Freud as half showman, half shaman, reporting his own nightly excursions. Sorrow, like guilt, never ends though it ebbs and flows. I have never 'got over' Raphael's death; it sliced my life in two. I still grieve for him and for what he missed – what he misses every day. To leave Raphael behind, now as then, always means another wrench, the heartlessness of having to make my own mark. That slash across the car was emotional graffiti, as if I were wielding a sword as well as a pen, a vicious burst of anger at the world that was keeping me alive and had killed him. Only that futile violence could gesture at the enormous pain of leaving the dead behind and the glee at doing so.

After Raphael died, people comforted me by saying that he would never grow old and my relationship with him would never now change. After more than twenty years the opposite seems true to me: he goes on changing in my inner life as I age and change. Once I dreamt that I met him in the street and thought, 'Oh Lord, he's been here all the time and I've gone and married again, what will he think?' For a while, in a reverie I imagined him meeting John and how they would take to each other in a parallel universe (Raphael was always soft on the Irish). And felt sad when I shook myself awake.

That part of me that lived with Raphael and loved him is unaccommodated still. But in one version of my endless dreams I find number 19 glamorously done up with lots of extra rooms, a garden and a fabulous modern kitchen, perhaps even – the final touch – a view of the sea. There is Raphael, in his newly refurbed study, buried in his books, puzzled by my concern. The past improved, expanded into the future, made over as if the unconscious were an interior decorator. And Raphael, somewhere in time, is still at work on retrofitting, and very much at home.

★

When I emerged, and I am still always emerging, from the shock of the meaninglessness of Raphael's death, and the accident of my own illness, I surely lost some recklessness. Loss is pure loss. I would say a 'black hole', if I was sure what that was, beyond some dark material that centrifugally swallows our certainties. What I have gained, on the other hand, is a proportionate sense of my own small, transient being and a quickening of the moment. I am less inclined to look forward and more grateful for, or convinced by, being here now. Still, though I shudder inwardly and cross my fingers for luck, I can't help but marvel at all those rushing headlong into their futures, all those blithe spirits full of nerve, lovers, dreamers, romantics all, who ride their wishes like wild horses, roughshod over the present, never looking back.

Envoi

Island of Ithaki, Greece, 15 September 2017

Last night I dreamt I was in Elder Street again. I was with friends and the rooms were slowly flooding but I was not alarmed. Far from it. I watched with Olympian calm as the house, from the basement up, began to fill with water. There was no sense of menace or any fear of drowning – only, as the water reached the first-floor sitting room, our 'room', where the sofa had been, I pointed out to my friends that all the old leather folios on the shelves, rows and rows of them as in a library, would soon be waterlogged and ruined. I was quite indifferent to this and woke refreshed.

Am I no longer feeling inundated by the past? No longer flooded with emotion? Or is the dream that wish? Here I am on this island, surrounded by water, in and out of it all day, but the desire to be rid of history, of the weight of books and words, to be somehow cleansed, I know that surfaced at different times in the marriage. Perhaps only now, as I imagine an end for the book I am writing, could I dream this dream. Not fire, but water. Not combustion, but suspension. Not the world turned upside down and ablaze with the revolution, but floating, embryonic. The library, with all its past, become an alembic, the alembic a womb.

Notes and Acknowledgements

In his beautiful memoir of his parents' lives, *Between Them*, the novelist Richard Ford advises his fellow memoirists not only to compose a shape but to find a 'reliable economy'. I have taken this to mean no academic paraphernalia, footnotes, bibliography and so on. I have tried to make any direct allusions to the works of other writers clear in the text. Since this book has been brewing for twenty-odd years, I cannot hope to share with the reader the many inspirations behind it, but I would like to mention a handful of books which left a mark on my own. My Spitalfields chapter benefited from my reading of Andrew Solomon's *The Noonday Demon: An Anatomy of Depression* and from Adam Phillips's work, particularly his essay 'On Success' in *On Flirtation* and his *Darwin's Worms*. *Spitalfields*, the encyclopaedic history written by my erstwhile neighbour Dan Cruickshank, taught me much of the history I did not know when I was living in the district; David Kynaston's fourth volume of *The City of London*, *A Club No More*, made sense of what was happening in the Square Mile during the 1980s and early 1990s. Sasha Abramsky's *The House of Twenty Thousand Books* is a loving tribute to his grandfather, Chimen Abramsky, Raphael's uncle, and helped me understand the fascinating and sometimes fraught worlds of Marxism and Jewish history as they mingled in Raphael's family. I must also single out Tom Laqueur's erudite and humane *The Work of the Dead: A Cultural History of Mortal*

Remains, and finally Tom Griffiths's *The Art of Time Travel: Historians and Their Craft*, which was very suggestive for thinking about archives and for much else touching on the role of the historian.

Raphael's essays on *The Lost World of British Communism* were reprinted by Verso in 2006 with a preliminary bibliography of his work and an initial list of his talks. Jean McCrindle's memoir 'The Hungarian Uprising and a Young British Communist' can be found in *History Workshop Journal*, vol. 62. 'Comers and Goers', Raphael's article on city itinerants, was published in H. J. Dyos and Michael Wolff's magnificent *The Victorian City: Images and Realities*, Volume 1, and 'The Pathos of Conservation', his account of Spitalfields as he knew it, with its sustained anger at the closing down of the market, is in *The Saving of Spitalfields*, published by the Spitalfields Historic Buildings Trust. The two volumes of Raphael's *Theatres of Memory: Past and Present in Contemporary Culture*, were also published by Verso. The second posthumous volume, *Island Stories*, has autobiographical material, as does *The Lost World*, and I have drawn on both.

This memoir is not an account of Raphael's work, but if you can find a copy of it, *History Workshop 1967–91*, Raphael's 'collectanea' of documents, is the best place to start for understanding how that movement within social history came about and what its ideals were. Raphael edited some two dozen books as a History Workshop series, and as a founding editor of *History Workshop Journal* he published innumerable articles and editorials in its pages. A virtual collection of his contributions to *HWJ* over the first two decades of its existence can be found at https://academic.oup.com/hwj/pages/raphaelsamuel. Sophie Scott-Brown's recent study, *The Histories of Raphael Samuel: A Portrait of a People's Historian*, sensitively explores the many nooks and crannies of his life and work. It also has a comprehensive bibliography. The Raphael Samuel Collection at the Bishopsgate Institute in London is open to all, and the activities of the History Centre established in his name can be found at www.raphaelsamuelhistorycentre.com. In 2016 the Centre kindly invited me to give the memorial lecture to mark the twentieth anniversary of Raphael's death, a chance to try out ideas for this book. The lecture was subsequently published in *History Workshop Journal*, vol. 83, and also led to a companion 'Diary' piece in the *London Review of Books*: my thanks to the editors and to the directors of the Centre.

There is no biography of Minna Keal, but more information about her life can be found on the sleeve notes of her CDs or online. A longer version of chapter 6, with more biographical detail, will be published online by the *Kenyon Review*. My thanks to the editor, David Lynn, and to Kate Kennedy and Katie Cooper at the Oxford Centre for Life-Writing at Wolfson College, which provided a lively occasion to talk about Minna.

I keep a toe in a number of academic institutions and am always glad of the support and stimulus I can rely on whenever I meet up with colleagues and students. I was especially fortunate to be able to complete the book amid congenial company as a Visiting Research Fellow at the Institute for Advanced Studies in the Humanities at the University of Edinburgh. I owe a debt to Simon Cooke of Edinburgh

University's English Department for the many animated conversations about memoir and for much else besides.

As ever I have found working with the team at Fig Tree/ Penguin a great pleasure. Warm thanks go to my editor Juliet Annan, who always knows when to leave me alone and when to intervene, and is always at the end of a phone line; my copy-editor, Caroline Pretty, worked her usual magic, spotting many slips and improving many sentences; Assallah Tahir kindly searched out permissions. Many years ago, David Godwin, my agent, urged me to write more about Raphael and, while it has taken longer than either of us might have wished, his continued confidence in my work has been crucial.

I'm also grateful to all those who answered my queries, large and small, impersonal and personal: to Joanna Bulli-vant, for generously sharing her considerable knowledge of music and British radical politics; to Rachel O'Higgins, to the late Edith Schlesinger, and to Carla Mitchell, Sue Dudman, David Mercer, Peter Swaab and Cora Kaplan. Jake Bharier, Raphael's cousin in Herefordshire, passed on help-ful information about the Samuel family, as did Roma and Melvyn Brooks in Israel. My sister, Sandra Pidoux, cast a weather eye over some of the tricky passages to do with my own family and offered her memories. Marybeth Hamil-ton and Fran Bennett perused early chapters of the manuscript and gave me heart; Kasia Boddy made careful comments on chapters 3 and 6, prompting some necessary rewriting; and at the eleventh hour Margaret Drabble read the whole thing and encouraged me over the finishing line. All the blunders and infelicities, of course, remain mine and mine alone.

Finally, my thanks go to my dear husband, John, who made his peace with Raphael's ghost long ago. He has read every word of this book or let me read it to him, and he always spurred me on. *A Radical Romance* is dedicated to him: 'the second time around', as 'Ol' Blue Eyes' once sang, is every bit as good.